NOT SUCH AN ASS

Also by Henry Cecil

★

BRIEF TO COUNSEL
Illustrated by Edward Ardizzone

★

Not Such an Ass

BY

HENRY CECIL

With a Foreword by
THE RT. HON. LORD JUSTICE DEVLIN
*one of the members of Her Majesty's
Court of Appeal in England*

HUTCHINSON OF LONDON

Fiction
Cecil

HUTCHINSON & CO. (*Publishers*) LTD
178–202 Great Portland Street, London, W.1

London Melbourne Sydney
Auckland Bombay Toronto
Johannesburg New York

★

First published 1961

© Henry Cecil 1961

*This book has been set in Baskerville type face. It has
been printed in Great Britain by The Anchor Press,
Ltd., in Tiptree, Essex, on Antique Wove paper and
bound by Taylor Garnett Evans & Co., Ltd., in
Watford, Herts*

Contents

Foreword

By The Rt. Hon.
LORD JUSTICE DEVLIN

Many people who come up against the law and lawyers find them both unsatisfactory and come away with a lot of questions they would like to have answered. This book is written for such people. Why should a man have to pay to get acquitted? If nobody can tell a man what the law is until his case has been decided, why should he be made to pay for having to find out? If a man will not pay his debts, is it any good sending him to prison? He will not earn any money there and it will be his wife and children who will suffer. Is it really true that the police cannot detain people for questioning and, if so, ought not someone to be able to do it: if a man is innocent why should he mind? If a criminal trial goes wrong on a technicality, why cannot there be another one? Why do cases take so long to come on for trial?

These are some of the questions that Mr Cecil discusses, and he shows that there are two sides to most of them. While he believes that English law and justice is essentially sound, he is not out to over-emphasise the 'not' in the title that he has chosen for this book; and he has plenty of new ideas. The sound

7

point that he makes throughout is that often new ideas
cost money and that if the public wants the best service,
it may have to pay more for it. Take, for example, the
law's delays. There is really no reason why a case
should not be heard as soon as it is ready for trial and
an appeal as soon as it is entered. They will have to be
heard sooner or later; and it does not cost any more
money to hear them sooner than later. Mr Cecil gives
good reasons for thinking that in the County Courts a
happy state of equilibrium has now been reached
between the number of cases ready to be tried and the
number of judges available to try them. In the High
Court throughout this century there has been a lag and
as soon as the judiciary seems to be catching up on
arrears, the volume of litigation increases. A few years
ago less than six months elapsed before an appeal
from the Queen's Bench was heard; now it is nearly
twelve. For trials also the waiting period has grown
longer. So the Government has acted and there is now
a Bill before Parliament for the appointment of six new
judges of the High Court and three new Lords Justices
of Appeal, an increase of about a fifth and a third
respectively. That will not cost very much money—
£72,000 less tax—and is not a new idea.

What would be an entirely new idea and undoubtedly cost much more money would be if Parliament, when it appointed an additional judge, were
also to provide an additional Court for him to sit in,
room for him to work in and accommodation for his
clerk. The Royal Courts of Justice in London were
built eighty years ago. They are described under the
head of Architecture in the *Encyclopaedia Britannica* as

'a costly failure', 'badly planned' and 'a warning how real architectural talent and vigour may be stultified by a sentimental adherence to a past phase of architecture'. As recently as the 1950s, as I can testify, there was also a sentimental adherence to a past phase of plumbing expressing itself in the ewer and basin with which every judge was provided and which had to be filled and emptied daily. Immense credit is due to the ingenuity of those who have succeeded in cramming the present judiciary into a building 'badly planned' for half the number; they will not be forgotten for they have a monument, apparently perdurable, in the shacks in the East Quadrangle erected to provide two Courts for what was supposed to be the transient flood of litigation after the 1914–1918 war.

We cannot go on indefinitely curing the law's delays by an Act of Parliament appointing more judges. Sooner or later—later no doubt, for there are other more urgent needs—we shall have to face the fact that London certainly and most provincial cities as well need more and better Courts. When that time comes there are two things that will be worth considering. The first is that the principle that all trials should take place in public, fundamental though it is, is hardly worth preserving if when the public come to Court they cannot hear a word of what anybody is saying. If that defect cannot be remedied by better design and acoustics, there is always the amplifier. The other thing is that the Treasury may reasonably object to putting up expensive buildings that are in use for less than three-quarters of the year. Is it necessary for the proper organization of the business of the High

Court that all judges should be on vacation at the same
time?

But I am only adding to the sort of questions that
Mr Cecil asks and answers about the administration of
justice. What is at the bottom of this book is Mr
Cecil's belief that the public is entitled to ask questions
about the working of the law and that they should be
answered in a way that it can understand. I share that
belief. The administration of the law is a public service
and the more questions the public asks about it the
better it is likely to be. Mr Cecil uses his skill as a
novelist to present the law in action to the ordinary man
in a way that he will find satisfying as well as amusing.

Patrick Devlin

1 *Nothing Like Justice*

ONE day judges and counsel may be abolished and replaced by electronic brains. The Royal Courts of Justice will become rather like an amusement arcade and litigants will be directed by signposts to the machine which deals with their particular type of dispute. They will put their various contentions into a slot and, after a suitable interval and perhaps a rumble of some kind, the answer will be deposited in a receptacle for the purpose.

There will be no question of an appeal, for Jackie (as the machine will be known from its initials J.A.C.C.[1]) will be infallible, or at any rate as infallible as man-made machines can be. If the machine should go wrong and in reply to the question 'does Brown owe Jones £135 10s. 6d.?' deliver a judgment 'six months' imprisonment each', no doubt there will be provision for going to another machine, while an attendant immediately puts up an 'out of order' notice on the offender.

This would be pleasantly reminiscent of the story that a Queen's Bench Court once had such a notice outside it when the judge was sitting. There were unkind people who maintained that the notice did not simply refer to the door on which it was hanging.

[1] Judicial Administration (Contested Cases).

Possibly the machines would speak instead of delivering written judgments. Or they might speak in the simplest and deliver reserved judgments in the more difficult cases. And, of course, there is no reason why, eventually, as electronic technique improves, they might not be able to deliver judicial homilies—or at least to keep the parties in suspense by reciting the facts at length before announcing the decision, thus falling into line with the strange thoughtlessness of some otherwise excellent human judges.

But if this should ever happen, will it be an improvement on the present system? Well, if the machines were always right, there would undoubtedly be more certainty in legal matters. But the difficulty seems to be that, in order to achieve this degree of infallibility, the machines would have to be constructed not simply by engineers but by lawyers of hitherto unknown excellence. So for the moment it looks as though the public must resign itself to our present methods of legal administration with such improvements as may take place from time to time.

In *Brief to Counsel* an attempt was made to indicate what was implied by a career at the Bar and to offer some elementary suggestions for the assistance of those embarking on that career. The object of the present book is partly to deal with some of the legal problems which face the public and the practitioner, and partly to give illustrations of some aspects of the law which are not generally known to the public. A week seldom goes by without a complaint, however small, being made of an apparent injustice. It is, therefore, of importance that the nature of the problems, and the

NOTHING LIKE JUSTICE 13

difficulties of solution, should be appreciated. The solution sometimes lies with the public, sometimes with the legal profession, sometimes with both—and sometimes there appears to be no solution at all. But, even when there is no solution, an appreciation of the circumstances which give rise to this unfortunate situation may at least be of some use and help to make the occasion less frustrating. Moreover, it may be a consolation, however slight, to know what the patient is suffering from. A cure may be round the corner.

It is perhaps a tribute to the standard of justice which exists in this country that the British public expects so much from its lawyers and judges. Although any fairly intelligent person would admit that he could not expect a judge or a lawyer never to make mistakes, the general impression which the public as a whole conveys by its reactions of indignation when something goes wrong is that it ought never to have happened. Indeed it might horrify some members of the public if they appreciated that no country's legal system can provide absolute justice or anything like it. Improvements are taking place all the time, but the desired goal is wholly unattainable.

The public does not expect to be able to go to the moon for the week-end just yet, but it does expect a man who is in the right to obtain everything to which he is entitled. The English system of justice has been the envy of many foreigners for generations and it is of a very high standard. Nevertheless, in matters of law in this country, a man who is in the right hardly ever gets everything to which he is entitled. It is an object of this book to explain why this is so and, when possible, to put forward suggestions for an improvement.

The three main reasons for dissatisfaction with the legal administration in any country are (1) delay and inconvenience, (2) uncertainty and (3) expense. No system of law has yet been invented by man which did not inevitably suffer from each of these defects. The best that can be done is to mitigate them. The important thing is, however, that at no time in a country's history should such defects be complacently accepted.

The greater part of this book deals with problems arising in connection with civil rights and litigation, but the next five chapters are devoted to problems relating to crime and the criminal law. The first of them is an extremely difficult problem which the public appears resolutely determined not to face. Judges call attention to it from time to time but apparently no one in authority has ever yet sought to deal with it.

2 *Detained for Questioning*

ONE Christmas day a number of men, who were suspected of a crime, were taken separately to a police station for questioning just before their Christmas dinner. The only one who did not protest vehemently turned out to be the culprit.

There are not many adults who still think that the methods adopted by the Criminal Investigation Department to find out who has committed a particular crime are those of Sherlock Holmes or those employed by many writers of detective stories. In the case of murder or some very serious crime, a vast number of enquiries may be made, but when some house or factory has been broken into, or some crime of that kind has taken place (and stealing and allied crimes form the vast majority of offences), there are two normal methods of tracing the offender. Usually they are combined. If they fail, then in most cases the criminal gets away with it.

The first method is 'information received'. An informer (amateur or professional) tells the police who did it. (By an amateur informer is meant the wife or a friend of the criminal.) The police then go down and interview the man implicated; sometimes they ask him a few questions first, sometimes they take him straight off to the police station. In a large number of these

cases the man either confesses at once or makes a
number of statements which can be proved to be
untrue, and confesses later when the untruths are
pointed out to him.

The other method is to question any man whose
'signature' is left at the scene of the crime. Many
regular criminals have only one method of committing
a crime. For example, if they break into a house
they turn the place upside down out of pure malice, or
they leave everything untouched except the article
they want, or they help themselves to food and drink,
or they deliberately foul the place, and so on. If the
particular breaking is of sufficient importance, the
police will question, or collect for questioning, all the
men whose signature appeared on the scene of the
crime, and who could have committed it. With luck,
the guilty one admits it or convicts himself by telling
various lies. Some might think that it is extraordinary
how a guilty conscience affects men who, one would
have thought, had jettisoned their consciences years
before. The truth is that, in their case, conscience
simply means knowledge of guilt combined with fear
of being found out; not regret for their misdeeds, only
regret at the possibility of having to pay for them. It
was this method which was adopted on that Christmas
day.

Now the police have an extraordinarily difficult task
to perform in the detection of crime, and they are not
given by the law the weapons with which to perform it.
These detentions, when they really are detentions, are
wholly illegal. Apart from certain statutory cases,
mostly concerned with motorists, the police have no

more right than anyone else to question people. You
could certainly knock at Bill Bloggins' door and start
to ask him a few questions. Provided you did not abuse
him or behave in a manner calculated to cause a
breach of the peace, there would be nothing illegal
about your conduct. Canvassers do it regularly during
an election. But if Mr Bloggins told you to go, you
would have to do so. If you were actually in or partly
in his house and you refused to go, he could push
you out, not using more force than was necessary. If
you were outside, he could slam the door in your face.
If you persisted in coming to call on him against his
will, he could eventually obtain an injunction to
restrain you from doing so, and it is you who would be
sent to prison if you defied the injunction.

Now (except in the case of the statutory exceptions
referred to) the police are in exactly the same position
as members of the public, and, if a man does not wish
to be questioned and tells them to go, they are in law
bound to do so. In the majority of cases the man's
conscience (as previously defined) makes him adopt a
more conciliatory attitude, and, indeed, when the
police ask or tell him to come along with them to the
station he often goes 'voluntarily'. In some cases it really
is voluntary, in others it is quite involuntary (i.e. he is
not given the chance to refuse, he is simply told to get
dressed and go with the police as though he were being
arrested) and in a number of cases it is half way
between the two. But when a man goes voluntarily it
is either because he thinks he is bound to do so or
because of his guilty conscience. In a television programme broadcast by the B.B.C. on 24th May 1960

B

and entitled 'Scotland Yard, a dramatised docu-
mentary about the Metropolitan Police' a detective-
inspector asked a man in a public house to go with
him to the police station. When the man demurred the
officer said he would take him. The man was not
arrested and the officer's behaviour was patently illegal.

Now it is very important from the public point of
view that, if crime cannot be prevented, it should be
detected and, unless the police adopted the methods
referred to, a very large number of crimes which are
today brought home to their perpetrators would be
committed with impunity. But what troubles some
people is the fact that, even though a substantial
number of suspects do go 'voluntarily' to the police
station for questioning, a number do not go voluntarily
at all and the whole basis of the method is illegal.

One can imagine the outcry there would be if a
perfectly respectable man were woken up in the middle
of the night and ordered by a police officer to come to
the police station with him. He would, no doubt, ask
if he were being arrested and, on being told he was
not, he would refuse point-blank and order the officer
out of his house. The next day he would consult his
solicitor, his Member of Parliament, and write to the
newspapers. Even if he were asked very politely if he
would mind going along to the police station to help
the police in their enquiries he would want to know why
next morning would not do. But, in fact, no police
officer would dream of ordering an obviously respectable person to come to the police station out of his
respectable home.

Occasionally a respectable person carrying a bag late

at night is asked by a police officer what he has in it. And what a hullabaloo this respectable person sometimes makes, instead of being glad that there was a police officer about at all and one who kept his eyes open. It is difficult to understand why these fierce, respectable people who complain at this sort of thing do not realize that the person stopped by the policeman might be a thief who had just stolen some of the fierce, respectable person's belongings. They would be pleased enough then that the man was stopped and made to open the bag.

But, although the fierce respectables complain bitterly about this sort of conduct, which is perfectly legal, few of them appear to mind at all when Bill Bloggins is detained for questioning. At any rate they do not write to the newspapers about it.

Is it satisfactory that the public as a whole should wink at an illegal practice, just because its object is a good one? Moreover, although in the vast majority of cases no threats or violence are used to induce the men to speak, in a small minority of cases violence or threats may be used. There is, of course, always the threat of the blue uniform which is automatically associated by criminals with prison, and accordingly questioning by a police officer is always conducted, however fairly, under the threat of prison. But in a small minority of cases it is alleged that violence or threats have been used and, if the allegations are true, there is obviously grave objection to confessions being obtained in that way. The difficulty is to ascertain whether they have been so obtained. Criminals quite often make allegations of this kind. Their word is not reliable, but they

may be speaking the truth. How is it possible to
ascertain with any certainty whether they are? In
many cases it is not, and, as the inception of the
questioning has often been illegal anyway, the situation
is far from satisfactory.

What, if anything, is to be done about it? With the
present increase of crime things would be even worse
if this illegal weapon were taken away from the police
and nothing substituted for it. Yet it is pretty unsatisfactory that the law-abiding public should accept as a
recognised method of detecting crime something which
everyone should know is illegal.

There is a solution to the problem, but it would offend
some people more than the present situation, which, it
must be conceded, does not appear to offend anyone
except a few lawyers. Criminals and potential criminals
have few spokesmen from among themselves. And,
indeed, complaints from guilty people about methods
employed to prove their guilt would not attract much
sympathy.

'Look, chum, see, I took the stuff all right. O.K. I
did. I'm guilty, see. But what do them rozzers want to
come and ask me about it for? It's up to them to find
out, ain't it? Why should I 'elp them? This is a free
country, ain't it? And if I pinch the stuff I oughter be
allowed ter keep it without 'aving a lot of grasshoppers
asking me questions. I don't like it, see. I ain't saying
they beat me up or anythink like that. But they took
me off to the station, see, and I ain't no scholard. So I
ain't got no chance with them asking me questions.
Anyway, I don't like it, see, and it's tiring after a day's
work, or a night's work, yer might say. Why didn't I

tell 'em to 'op it when they come for me? Nah, really,
guv! If two ruddy great coppers called on you, what
would you say? Oh, I forgot, guv. You're posh and that
makes the difference. But I like a quiet life. If no one
don't interfere with me, I don't interfere with them—
not personal-like, that is. And I go quiet, every time.
But it don't seem to be fair to 'ave to tell 'em all about
it. It ain't English, if yer see what I mean, guv.'

Such a complaint would not secure many sym-
pathisers, and, indeed, provided it were lawfully done,
and provided it did not lead to suspicion of worse
things, there is no great objection to suspects being
detained. It is bad luck on a man who is completely
innocent, but, provided he is not detained for longer
than is absolutely necessary and is treated with
consideration during his detention, no great harm
would normally be done. But such a solution, i.e. the
mere legalisation of the present situation, would be
totally unacceptable to most people, as it would put
too much legal power in the hands of the police. It
would mean, for example, that the respectable, if
obstinate, old gentleman who refuses to show the
contents of his suitcase to a constable could be taken
into custody at once. It would mean that, if a policeman
took a dislike to anyone, he could invent a story to
justify his detaining him. If there were enmity between
two men in the same street, and one of them were a
policeman, he could probably contrive to take the
other in custody to the station and even detain him
there for an hour or two before he was released. A
solution, therefore, needs to be found that will not put
too much power in the hands of the police but which

will at the same time give them sufficient power to deal with crime without employing illegal methods as they do at present.

It may be that there are defects in the solution suggested below or that there are more satisfactory alternatives. It is merely put forward as a suggestion with the object, not so much of having this particular idea adopted as of having the whole situation investigated thoroughly, so that one way or another the present practice may cease. Otherwise it will continue until there is some big public scandal which compels public action in the matter. It is far better that the practice should be abolished before this happens.

The reason why the solution which is now put forward will probably offend a substantial portion of the population, including lawyers, is the deeply inrooted idea in most people that no man is bound to make admissions against himself. In other words although, as has been seen, the words do not come very well from the miscreant himself, the average person does not like the idea of a man being compelled to convict himself by his own admissions. The origin of this dislike is perhaps the fact that there was a time, centuries ago, when torture was used to extract such confessions. It is not due to the dislike of the methods recently used in other countries. Long before the war there would have been just as much objection to a man being compelled to admit his guilt as there would be today.

If by 'compelled' torture or any similar means of compulsion is envisaged, obviously no one would even suggest such a method of proving guilt. But, in fact, what objection is there to a man being legally liable to be questioned before a responsible person, e.g. a justice of the peace, with a lawyer present to safeguard his interests, if he is suspected of crime? If a man has in fact committed a crime what is there so terrible in asking him about it and using his answers in evidence against him, provided no violence or threat of violence or any similar pressure is put upon him? At the moment the police often quite illegally take a man off to a police station and question him. Would it not be far better if the police had power, on reasonable suspicion, to convey a man *immediately* before a justice of the peace where he could be lawfully questioned? There could be a panel of justices available at all times of the day and night and a panel of solicitors and barristers available to attend on the man's behalf if a lawyer of his own choosing were not available. Provision could be made that nothing said by the person questioned would be evidence *against* him, unless it was said either during the commission of a crime or a chase after it or unless it was said before a justice of the peace. This would prevent the slightest suspicion that statements made by accused persons had been procured by threats or violence. If the person concerned refused to answer, it could be provided (1) that such refusal could be given in evidence against him and/or (2) that, if he is tried for an offence, he should be presumed guilty unless and until he proved his innocence.

Such a suggestion may strike horror into the minds of many people who are used to the burden of proving guilt being upon the prosecution. So it has been for hundreds of years. So it would remain if the man questioned answered the questions. But why should a guilty man shelter behind silence? What is the legal or moral objection, provided proper safeguards are used, to a man being liable to convict himself out of his own mouth? After all, if he is not guilty, he won't do so. It is only the guilty people who will suffer. And why shouldn't they? They suffer now in precisely that way, but the procedure used against them is often illegal and lends itself to gross abuse.

It is true that there might be a few obstinate but innocent people who refused to answer questions. The penalty for their obstinacy would be that later on they would have to prove their innocence.

It would have to be provided that a police officer would have to have reasonable grounds for taking the man before a justice of the peace, and, if he did not, he and his superiors would be liable to an action for damages. Such a provision and the fact that the man would be taken before a justice of the peace and not just to the police station should be enough to prevent the abuse of power, which would be the danger of merely legalising the present procedure.

It will be said that, if confessions are going to be obtained, it is important that there should be no delay. That is in many cases true. And that is why the police collect people sometimes at night or just before their Christmas dinner. That is the reason why it would be necessary to have justices of the peace and lawyers available at any time of the day or night. There would be no difficulty in obtaining the statistics to see how many justices of the peace and how many lawyers would be required to be available in each district.

Such a change in the law is most improbable, for the reasons indicated. Many people who sit back quietly, and make no complaint whatever of the illegal methods at present adopted by the police, would complain bitterly at the idea that Bill Sykes should have to answer questions or prove his own innocence. It is very doubtful if such a suggested change will ever get as far as a Bill in Parliament because of this deep-rooted feeling. But how would each individual objector answer the questions:

'Then do you approve of the present illegal methods adopted, do you desire them to be continued and, if not, what are you going to do about it?' For it is certain that, if the police were simply prohibited from using the present system without any powers being given to them in substitution, undetected crimes would continue to increase on a much larger scale. One of the main weapons held by the police would have been taken away and nothing done to replace it.

This leads quite naturally to a consideration of the present wave of crime. There is one way and one way only to reduce this substantially within the next couple of years. And it is not by the increase of penalties or the introduction of new ones. It is true that one of the reasons why some people continued to steal in spite of the death penalty was because they had to steal to live, and they preferred to risk immediate execution rather than death by starvation. But, if the death penalty were re-introduced for stealing, there would still be burglars, even though today no one need starve. That is because man is naturally an optimist and, however often a man may have been caught in the past, he always assumes that he will not be caught next time. And, indeed, even in the case of men who are convicted every year except when they are actually in prison, they no doubt commit a large number of crimes for which they are not caught.

There is only one thing which would reduce and prevent crime, and that is a very substantial increase in the police force. If the pay of the police were to be doubled there would most certainly be a considerable increase in the detection of crime and, better still, an increase in the prevention of it.

That involves the question of finance. Can the country afford it? What are the priorities? At least the public should recognise that the only solution to certain problems is the spending of more public money. And if they want to reduce crime substantially, they will have to spend it. Unquestionably it is very important to improve prison conditions and to help to reform criminals, but one would have thought that, unless there were sufficient money to do everything at the same time, the first thing to be tackled was the immediate reduction of crime. And, if the bold step were taken of making a position in the police force one of the most sought-after jobs, not just by adding something to its pay but by doubling it, that reduction would swiftly take place.

.   .   .   .   .

Since this chapter was written the pay of the police force has been increased. It remains to be seen whether the increase is sufficient to have the desired effect.

3 *Criminal Appeals*

ONE of the questions which is raised from time to time, and upon which there is considerable divergence of opinion, relates to appeals from criminal convictions. Should the Court of Criminal Appeal have power to order a new trial if, for any reason, it thinks that the first trial has been unsatisfactory? Practically no one suggests that, if a man is acquitted, the prosecution should have a right to appeal and ask for a new trial. But, where a man has been convicted, lawyers and others have been arguing, ever since the Court of Criminal Appeal was created in 1907, whether the Appeal Court's power should be limited to allowing or dismissing the appeal or whether it should also have the right to order a new trial.

Indeed, when the Bill was before the House of Lords in 1907, the Lord Chancellor, Lord Loreburn, in deference to the view of 'high legal authorities', agreed to the provision of a power to order a new trial. That provision was struck out by the House of Commons and later the Lord Chancellor said he had allowed its insertion although it did not entirely correspond with his own judgment. He said that there was a great deal to be said for the action of the House of Commons because 'it approaches the confines of torture to put a man on trial twice for the same offence'.

It should, however, be borne in mind that, if this is a fair statement, the present law approaches those confines for, if a jury disagrees, a prisoner is normally retried once. Lord Loreburn did not voice any objection to that second trial. There is a practice (but it is not based on any rule of law) that, if a second jury disagrees, the prosecution offer no evidence and the accused is automatically acquitted on his third trial. There are, indeed, objections to a new trial being ordered if a jury disagrees on a first trial, but the arguments in favour of such a new trial outweigh those objections. There is a limit to the tenderness which should be shown to the man in the dock. And, in fact, that tenderness is not really meant particularly for him; it is to ensure, as far as possible, that no innocent man shall be found guilty. If, just because there is one obstinate person on a jury when the other eleven are convinced of the man's guilt, a man is to be entitled to be acquitted, then justice would be stretched far too much on the side of the criminal. But, if the prisoner is lucky enough to have an obstinate person in his favour twice on a jury, then the opinion of Lord Loreburn that it would 'approach the confines of torture' to try him a third time can properly be invoked.

So today a man may be tried twice but not three times, although it must be emphasised that this is the practice, not the law. Theoretically, he could be tried an indefinite number of times. And theoretically it would be possible to have a prisoner who demanded a third trial. Such a man might say:

'I want a full trial, so that I can be fairly and squarely acquitted, after all the evidence has been heard. I don't want it to be said hereafter that I was technically acquitted because two juries had disagreed. I am innocent and I want the chance of having this clearly demonstrated.'

As far as is known, no one has ever done this and it could be argued that this suggests that most of those automatically acquitted on a third trial must have thought themselves to be guilty. It may be argued that at least *one* intelligent person, who really knew himself to be innocent, would have made this protest and demanded a third trial. But perhaps this is expecting too much even of the innocent.

Should a person ever make this request for a third trial, presumably the prosecution would accede to it, though, if the third jury disagreed, it is very doubtful if in any circumstances a fourth trial would be agreed to. And the accused would have no right to demand it. If the prosecution offers no evidence, the jury must acquit, though it has been known for a jury for one reason or another (either because they had read about the case or took a dislike to the accused or were interested in hearing more) to refuse to take this course. Several times the judge told them that they must find the prisoner 'not guilty', as no evidence on which they could find him guilty had been forthcoming and the burden was on the prosecution to prove guilt, not on the accused to prove innocence; but the jury obstinately refused to do what they were told and eventually the judge had to discharge them. A new and more reasonable jury was empanelled and duly acquitted the prisoner.

The fact that one member of a jury can prevent that

jury from convicting a prisoner makes one wonder
whether there has ever been impersonation of a juryman in a trial which has not attracted much publicity.
The fear of discovery would probably be too great in a
much publicised case but, in the ordinary criminal
trial which the Press does not normally bother to
report, it is not impossible that a juryman has been
approached by a stranger (in fact a friend of the
accused) and asked if he'd like the day off. After all,
sitting on a jury is very burdensome to many jurymen
and involves a number of them in severe financial loss.
No one knows any of them by sight and it would be
fairly simple for Mr X of such and such an address to
give his necessary particulars to the kindly stranger
and go off to his business. The danger, of course, is
that, if the would-be impersonator chose the wrong
juryman, who pretended to fall in with his suggestions
and then informed the authorities, he would be caught
and, no doubt, given a very heavy sentence.

The actual wording of that last phrase is of some
interest. It will be observed that the trial of the would-
be impersonator is completely omitted. The man's guilt
is assumed and the only matter considered is his punishment. Apart from such questions as pyschological
treatment in the punishment of offenders and of
rehabilitation and the like (which are not matters with
which this book is concerned) the only question people
consider when it is stated (as above) that a man has
committed a crime, is how serious is the crime and what
should be the punishment. But, put that man in the
dock and charge him with the crime, and immediately
nearly everything is done to assist in his acquittal.

The reason for this is the public fear that an innocent man may be convicted and no other method of minimising this risk has yet been devised. In other words, the only known method of trying to prevent injustice of this kind is to make the meshes of the net so wide that many guilty fish will escape with the innocent. But that is, of course, injustice itself. It is not justice for a guilty man to be acquitted, although that kind of injustice is probably preferred throughout all the civilised world to the other. It certainly is preferred here. The people who are in most danger of being convicted of serious crimes of which they are innocent are confirmed criminals and men with a bad criminal record. Then there is a danger of injustice. A man may be committing one crime when another is committed and, if he is suspected of the crime which he has not committed, he is not very likely to give the truthful alibi—which would not be of much use to him. So he lies about his whereabouts at the time of the crime of which he is innocent, and the police are able to prove that his statements are lies. 'Why should he lie if he were innocent?' asks the prosecution, and it is doubtful if any defending counsel has ever been bold enough to argue in reply:

'Well, he may have been committing another crime and not like to say.'

Of course, if the one crime were capital murder and the other merely safebreaking, no doubt the true alibi would be proved.

In considering, therefore, this question whether there should be power in the Appeal Court to grant a new trial, it is right to bear in mind, as one of the factors,

that very few innocent people of good character are
ever charged before a jury with a serious offence (other
than motoring offences) and the number of convictions
of such people of serious crime is probably infinitesimal.
On the other hand, of course, the greatest care should
be taken not to allow persons of bad character to be
convicted of crimes which they have not committed.
It is, however, fair to say that it is in the highest degree
improbable that the question of ordering a new trial
will arise in the case of an innocent man of good
character. If a prisoner is in fact guilty, and has been
found guilty once by a jury, there is no need to be too
unhappy about ordering a new trial if some legal mistake has been made during the first trial. Furthermore,
if a prisoner is a man of bad character who has already
experienced several trials when he has been found
guilty, it is unlikely that one extra trial will do him
much harm.

There are two main arguments in favour of giving
the Court the power of ordering a new trial. The first
is that it is not right (if it can be avoided) that a man
should escape the just consequences of his crime merely
because some mistake has been made at his trial, and
the second is that there are cases where the Appeal
Court might be prepared to order a new trial, but is not
prepared to quash the conviction. The first argument is
for the protection of the public, the second for the
assistance of convicted people. The first argument
certainly appears to be the more important. It is quite
true that the Appeal Court has the power to dismiss an
appeal in spite of a mistake during the trial, if satisfied
that there has been no miscarriage of justice. But this

power is used sparingly and the Court will not put itself in the position of the jury. Accordingly, unless it can feel quite sure that a jury would have convicted if the mistake had not been made, it is bound to allow the appeal.

A few years ago, owing to certain decisions of the Court of Criminal Appeal, and judicial statements made in the course of those decisions, some High Court judges did not feel at all sure how to express to the jury the measure of proof in criminal cases. For many years the proper direction had been said to be that the jury must be satisfied beyond all reasonable doubt. But for a time this direction was rather disapproved by the Court of Criminal Appeal, and it was said that juries should be told that they must 'feel sure' of the prisoner's guilt or that some similar suitable expression should be used. The Court said that it was difficult to explain what 'beyond all reasonable doubt' meant, and that the attempts of some judges to explain it might have confused the jury.

It was perhaps not fully appreciated by the Court which made these criticisms of the 'beyond all reasonable doubt' direction (which had satisfied judges and juries for very many years) that it is just as difficult to explain what 'feeling sure' means. If a juryman had asked: 'My Lord, how sure have I to be?'

JUDGE: You have to be quite sure. You must know what that means.

JURYMAN: Well, I'm afraid I don't, my Lord. I'm quite sure I can see your Lordship. Have I to be as sure as that?

JUDGE: Of course not.

C

JURYMAN: Then by 'quite sure' your Lordship seems
to mean 'not quite sure'.

At any rate, as a result of the criticisms of the 'beyond
all reasonable doubt' direction, some High Court
judges became uncertain how to sum up, with the
result that eventually a murder case came before the
Court of Criminal Appeal where there was plainly
some doubt as to the measure of proof which the jury
had been told they must adopt. As the defence was that
the prisoner had not intended to kill, it was quite vital
that the measure of proof should have been clearly laid
down and it was not. In consequence the appeal was
allowed and the accused man went free. Not long
afterwards he was charged with another offence.

Now it was plainly undesirable that, *if* the accused
was in fact guilty of murder, he should have been
allowed to go free just because the judge had made a
mistake in summing up. The justice of such a case
required that, if he could be tried *fairly* again, the man
should be tried again and a proper direction given to the
jury on his second trial. A substantial number of cases
where appeals are allowed are cases of that kind. They
are cases where a man is probably, or even very probably,
guilty and where a jury has been satisfied of his guilt
beyond all reasonable doubt, for that is once again the
normal direction used. Accordingly it seems wrong that
the men should go free just because of a mistake. The
public interest must be considered both ways. The first
consideration may well be that innocent men should
not be convicted, but a second is that guilty people
should not be allowed to cock a snook at the law and
be free to commit further crimes, without at least

having been punished for the crimes of which they were guilty.

It should also be remembered that in parts of the British Commonwealth new trials can be ordered and the law there appears to work satisfactorily.

The most important objection to the ordering of a new trial after a conviction is the possibility that it will not be fair. There are various other objections which were dealt with in the debates when the 1907 Bill was being discussed in Parliament and they may be summarised in the speeches of Lord Coleridge and Sir John Walton, the Attorney-General. Lord Coleridge said:

There are obvious objections to this course (new trial) on the score of delay, on the score of being unable to get together the witnesses and on the score of expense.

Sir John Walton said that:

Broadly speaking the new court was only asked to do what the Home Office had been doing for years—to see whether convictions were to be maintained or set aside. It was in his opinion most desirable that no new development should take place in any Criminal Court, that the State should not be put to the cost of putting all that machinery right for the second ordeal and that witnesses should not be subject to the trouble and the prisoner to the ordeal of a second trial. . . . Was it desirable that, having once tried and once convicted a person under such painful circumstances, they should go through all that form again in the interests of some abstract standard of justice? It was perfectly clear that no new trial could be ordered unless there was serious doubt. . . . So that the very ground on which a new trial was ordered would entitle the accused to get clear upon the ground that the doubt existed. Apart from fresh facts defence of prisoners in these cases would be reduced to a formula. . . . Then in the case of fresh evidence was it wise to have a new trial with all the disadvantages of costs and difficulty attending that investigation? Practical difficulties in the way of providing for new trials was enormous: in the first instance a man could not be tried over again at his own expense but at the expense of the country. Witnesses must be kept— prevented from going abroad.

Of course there is great force in these arguments but the difficulties referred to all have to be faced when a man has to be tried again after a jury has disagreed on the first trial. It is true that in very long cases, where the Appeal Court could not hear the appeal for some time, the delay would be longer and difficulties in regard to witnesses increased. But the only difference between the second trials which take place today and the second trials which many judges think the Appeal Court should have the power of ordering is that some delay would be involved. Otherwise the circumstances would be exactly the same. Is this one difference sufficient to make a second trial proper in the one case and not in the other?

Many people think that this depends upon whether the second trial is likely to be fair. Now this difficulty arises to some extent in the case of any second trial today where there has been great publicity from the first. The jury may have read the evidence in the newspapers. This objection is very close to the objection that proceedings in Magistrates' Courts should not be reported lest the trial jury may be prejudiced. Although now there is power for magistrates to exclude the public and the Press if they think fit, it is a power which is very rarely exercised and, in one of the famous cases where the accused might have been prejudicially affected by the reports of the magisterial proceedings, he was in fact acquitted.

But there is one essential difference between Press reports where a jury has disagreed and reports where a man has been convicted. In the latter case the prisoner will have been sentenced and, if he has previous convictions, they will have been read out in Court, and reported in the Press. It has long been recognised by lawyers that, in the average case, it is deadly from the point of view of a prisoner for the jury to know that he has previous convictions, particularly for the same type of offence as that with which he is being charged. Very occasionally they have to be made known, or, indeed, the prisoner's counsel brings them out because they *help* his case. But those cases are exceptional. Every judge and barrister would accept that, in the average case, it is of the highest importance that the jury should not know of a man's previous convictions. And if, by accident, mention is made of one during the trial, the jury will normally be discharged and the trial will start all over again before a fresh jury.

In these circumstances, if a case has been widely or even moderately publicised, and the convictions of the accused have been read out in open court, there is either a certainty or a probability that at least one of the jury on a second trial will have read about these previous convictions. Although a judge might warn a jury that they must disregard such matters it is difficult to maintain that such a trial would be fair. That is why, if an accidental disclosure of previous convictions is made during a trial, a new trial is usually ordered.

Now it is presumably a complete answer to the creation of a power to grant a new trial to show that it is unlikely that the new trial will be fair. And, if the second jury knew of earlier convictions, it is not likely that the second trial would be fair. It is quite true that in many cases of no particular interest there would be no Press reports at all and that in many other cases the reports would only be in the local Press. But unquestionably there would be some cases where the national Press carried a full report. In cases of merely local publicity the difficulty might be overcome by ordering the second trial to take place in a locality far away from that of the local newspapers which carried the report. But in the case of national publicity there would appear to be no method of ensuring that the second trial would be fair, if the convicted man had previous convictions.

Is this objection then conclusive that the power to order a new trial must not be given to the Court because, in some cases, a second trial would not be fair? When Abraham begged God to spare Sodom and Gomorrah if fifty decent people could be proved to live there, and God agreed, Abraham gradually reduced the number to ten, and God would have spared the city for that number. 'Wilt Thou also destroy the righteous with the wicked?' asked Abraham. It is perhaps not very accurate to refer to the vast bulk of those who come up against the criminal law as righteous (although a large number of the wicked are acquitted and so presumed righteous), but, subject to that comment, it

would seem right to suggest that if some people, however few, would not get a fair second trial if the law
were changed, then the change should not be made,
unless some method of avoiding this unfairness can be
suggested.

Can such a method be devised? It is suggested that
it can.

Although in murder cases, where the penalty is fixed,
the character of the accused need never be mentioned,
in other cases it has to be. And it would be hopelessly
unsatisfactory to prohibit reports in the Press of previous
convictions until an appeal (or second trial) had been
disposed of or the time for appealing expired. One
reason alone is enough to dispose of this possibility. It
is important that the public should feel satisfied as to
the justice of sentences and, if they were not allowed
to know the character of the prisoners being sentenced
until weeks afterwards, they could not possibly be so
satisfied in many cases.

But, if new trials were introduced, a possible solution
of the problem just mentioned is this. In any case
where there was local or national publicity the appellant
could have the option of having his appeal heard as it
is at present on the legal principles now existing,
without the possibility of a new trial being ordered or,
if and only if *he* preferred to have the chance of a new
trial, he could ask for the appeal to be heard on the
basis that a new trial could be ordered. Accordingly,
if he or his advisers felt that a new trial would not be
fair, it could be provided that, on the production of any
newspaper containing matter which could unfairly
prejudice a second trial, he would be entitled as of

right to have his appeal heard and determined as
appeals are heard today. The choice would be entirely
the appellant's, and accordingly in such cases he would
certainly be no worse off than he is today and, indeed,
he would be better off because he would have the
additional right to ask for a new trial if he preferred it.

It may be that, where there was only *local* publicity,
the appellants' right should be limited to choosing the
place of the new trial and that the right to demand
that the appeal should be determined on present-
day principles should be restricted to cases where
there was national publicity, but this is a matter for
argument.

But subject to this, it is suggested that the adoption
of this solution would satisfactorily deal with the comparatively small number of cases where a second trial
might not be fair.

The second argument for giving the Court power to
order a second trial was put forward by Mr Salter
(later Mr Justice Salter) when the 1907 Act was being
debated as a Bill. He said *that the Court of Criminal Appeal
would be much more likely to listen to cases if they had the
power to order a re-trial.*

Mr Salter did not mean that the Court would be
unlikely to hear cases properly if that power were not
given to them, but that, in some cases where the Court
would today dismiss an appeal, it might be prepared
to order a new trial if the appellant wanted it. This
argument has since then been advanced by others.

The fact is that not only in 1907 and 1908, but later
in 1948 and 1952, eminent judges expressed themselves
strongly in favour of the power to order a new trial

being given to the Court of Criminal Appeal. Eminent judges are not always right (it was pointed out in the Debate[1] in 1869, about imprisonment for debt, that they were against the abolition of execution for stealing) but there has now been over fifty years' experience of the Court of Criminal Appeal, and, if the general judicial view is that the power should be given, and if the method of dealing with the possibility of unfairness suggested above is considered a possible solution of that difficulty, it is perhaps time that the matter was reconsidered.

In 1952 in the debate in the House of Lords ten peers spoke, and nine of them, including the Lord Chancellor and the Lord Chief Justice, spoke in favour of this additional power being granted to the Court. The main argument of Lord Simon, who spoke on the other side, was that the second trial would not be fair. That, too, was the view of Lord du Parcq, although he did not speak during the debate. But the above suggestion for dealing with the possibility of unfairness was at no time put forward.

Here is an entirely fictitious case which may serve to make clearer to non-lawyers the principles involved. The scene is Mr and Mrs William Brown's bed-sitting room:

BROWN: They'll be 'ere soon. I know they will. Nah —don't forget—when they come. . . . I was with you all the time. In bed. You woke up because you 'ad a 'eadache or somefink. Yus, and yer looked at the clock. Don't ferget. It was twenty past one—and I was 'ere next to you. Asleep.

[1] Page 149 *post*.

Mrs Brown: P'raps they won't come this time after all. 'Ow should they know it was you?

Brown: Dunno, but they always seems to. Only two big jobs I got away with in the last ten years. It makes yer fink.

Mrs Brown: 'Aven't I told you it ain't worth it? Any straight job is better than this.

(There is a knock at the door)

Brown (in a whisper): Don't forget—yer looked at the clock.

(Another slightly louder knock)

Orl right, orl right. I'm coming.

(Brown opens the door)

Inspector Burke: Is that him, Sergeant?

Sergeant James: That's him, Inspector.

Brown: What's it orl about? I don't know yer.

Sergeant James: No, but you know me. This is Inspector Burke. Can we come in?

Brown: Well—wotcher want?

(They all go into the house)

Inspector: We'd like to ask you a few questions. This is Mrs Brown, I presume?

Mrs Brown: Yes—and none the best pleased for seeing you. Can't call one's 'ome one's own.

Brown: Let 'em be, Liz. The sergeant's orl right, but wotcher want an inspector for? I ain't done nothink.

Inspector: Who said you had?

Brown: Well, when yer come busting into a lady's bedroom I don't reckon you're on a paper chase.

Sergeant: What d'you think we want to ask you about?

BROWN: No idea. I wos in bed.

INSPECTOR: What d'you mean—you were in bed? When were you in bed?

BROWN: All the time. The missus can vouch for it. Can'tcher?

MRS BROWN: Course I can. I'd just looked at the clock—I'd got a 'eadache—it said 1.20.

INSPECTOR: You're sure it's right?

MRS BROWN: Course I am. As a matter of fact, I timed it by the wireless last night.

INSPECTOR: Well, well. And what made either of you think that we were interested in something which happened at 1.20 last night—or perhaps I should say this morning?

BROWN: You arst me, didn'tcher?

INSPECTOR: Oh, no, we didn't. We haven't said anything happened yet. Mind if we have a look round? I haven't got a search warrant—but I could get one.

BROWN: Do wotcher like.

SERGEANT: What time did you go to bed, Bill?

BROWN: Ten o'clock.

SERGEANT: Listen to the wireless?

BROWN: No.

SERGEANT: Thought you might have. They've got a programme just up your street. 'This is the Law.' 'Housebreaking.'

BROWN: Funny, arn'tcher.

SERGEANT: There are worse things than housebreaking.

INSPECTOR: Here, what's this?

BROWN: It's my . . . (Pause)

INSPECTOR: Well? Is it *your* cap? (Pause) Well—is it?

MRS BROWN: Course it's 'is. I got it for 'im.

INSPECTOR: Did you; from whom?

MRS BROWN: Second-'and from a barrer boy.

INSPECTOR: Well, I'm going to borrow it, if you don't mind. Sure you were in bed between one and half past, Brown?

BROWN: Course I was—'ow often do I 'ave to tell yer?

INSPECTOR: Well, it'll be just as well for you if you were—because the night watchman at the Medway Warehouse was murdered just about then.

MRS BROWN: Murdered, did yer say?

INSPECTOR: Yes, ma'am, murdered.

MRS BROWN: Oh—my God.

INSPECTOR: And, for reasons which I won't mention at present, I have some ground for thinking this may be his cap—picked up in a hurry perhaps. I shall want you to come along to the station, Brown.

BROWN: I didn't do it, Liz. I swear I didn't.

So Bill Brown is taken off to the police station. Nothing very unusual in that. He'd been there a good many times in his 33 years, and been kept there most of them. Larceny, burglary, housebreaking, assault with intent to evade arrest. He was usually upset when they took him, but never so much as on this occasion. He hadn't been charged yet, but he could see it coming— murder. And it came.

INSPECTOR: William Brown, I charge you with the murder of Thomas Jones on the 1st June last. You are not obliged to say anything in answer to the charge unless you wish to do so, but I must warn you that

anything you do say will be taken down in writing and
may be given in evidence.

BROWN: I didn't do it. I swear it.

INSPECTOR: Would you like to make a statement as
to your movements that night?

BROWN: I've told you—I was in bed.

INSPECTOR: And that's all you wish to say?

BROWN: It's the truth.

Well, it wasn't the truth—far from it. On that particular night William Brown was engaged in robbing
the Medway Warehouse in company with two other
men—both in custody—Charles Grant and George
Richardson. But, as the sergeant had said, there are
worse things than warehouse-breaking. Someone murdered the night watchman. It was obviously one or
more or all of the three men arrested. But which? That
was for the prosecution to prove and here is part of the
speech of counsel for the Crown.

PROSECUTING COUNSEL: Members of the jury, both
the prisoners Grant and Richardson admitted to the
police when they were arrested that they were at the
scene of the crime but the other prisoner, Brown, says
he was in bed all the time. He has throughout persisted
in that denial. Now his Lordship will warn you that
nothing that the other prisoners said to the police is
evidence against Brown, but it is to be noticed that each
of them said that Brown was with them.

JUDGE: Mr Carstairs, that really is a most unfortunate way of introducing the matter. Please be more
careful. Members of the jury, kindly disregard what
counsel has last said to you. At the moment there is
absolutely no indication that the prisoner Brown was

on the scene at all. Mr Carstairs, when I refused an order for separate trials I assumed that the prosecution would be conducted with its usual fairness. If that kind of thing happens again, I shall discharge the jury and order separate trials.

CARSTAIRS: I'm extremely sorry, my Lord. It was quite unintentional.

So the case goes on, Mr Carstairs being more than usually careful not to offend again. The case against William Brown, however, becomes stronger as the evidence is given, particularly when the other two prisoners start calling evidence. They themselves give evidence that Brown was the ringleader of the gang and that neither of them had anything to do with the killing of the watchman. Of course, if what they say is true, Brown must be the murderer, but they are interested persons, and may very well be lying to save their own skins. But, unfortunately for Brown, the cap does turn out to be the night watchman's and his own was found at the warehouse. A little difficult for him now to say he wasn't there. Why should he be the only one of the three to deny that he was there? Because, say the prosecution, he has more to be frightened of than the other two. They may be guilty, too, even if they never struck the blow, but Brown's behaviour in denying that he was there at all might well make the jury think that he had more to hide. And then, as the case is mounting against Brown, a Miss Bell is called to give evidence on behalf of George Richardson.

RICHARDSON'S COUNSEL: Is your full name Patricia Bell?

MISS BELL: Yes.

RICHARDSON's COUNSEL: And do you live at 14, Hornby Buildings, W.C.?

MISS BELL: I do.

RICHARDSON's COUNSEL: D'you know any of the prisoners?

MISS BELL: Not well. I've met them all.

RICHARDSON's COUNSEL: Did any of them speak to you on the 31st of May or thereabouts?

MISS BELL: The prisoner Brown spoke to me.

BROWN: That's a lie.

JUDGE: Be quiet. You are being defended by counsel who will fully protect your interests. Don't interrupt again.

RICHARDSON's COUNSEL: What did he say?

MISS BELL: He said they were going to do the Medway Warehouse the next night.

JUDGE: Did you know what that meant?

MISS BELL: I've been to the pictures, my Lord, and I thought he meant break into the place.

JUDGE: Very well.

RICHARDSON's COUNSEL: Did he say anything else?

MISS BELL: Yes. He said that if the night watchman gave any trouble—he'd get more than he gave.

BROWN: That's a lie.

JUDGE: I've spoken to you once. If you interrupt again, I shall postpone the hearing until tomorrow. You do yourself no good by these outbursts. You will have every opportunity if you wish of telling your own story in due course. In the meantime, you can speak to your solicitor or write down any instructions about this witness's evidence and give them to him. Go on, Mr Drake.

RICHARDSON's COUNSEL: When he said that, did he show you anything?

MISS BELL: Yes.

RICHARDSON's COUNSEL: What?

MISS BELL: A hammer.

RICHARDSON's COUNSEL: May the witness see Exhibit 1, my Lord, please? (Pause) Was it anything like that?

MISS BELL: I think that was it. It's exactly like.

RICHARDSON's COUNSEL: Thank you, Miss Bell.

JUDGE: Wait a moment, Miss Bell. Mr Brown's counsel wants to ask you some questions. Have you had sufficient instructions from your client to enable you to cross-examine, Mr Spooner?

BROWN's COUNSEL: My solicitor has taken them, thank you, my Lord. Now, Miss Bell, I suggest to you that your story is a tissue of lies from beginning to end.

MISS BELL: It's not; it's the truth!

BROWN's COUNSEL: I suggest to you that you've only met the prisoner Brown once in your life.

MISS BELL: Twice.

BROWN's COUNSEL: I suggest to you that you met him once three months before the murder and never again till now.

MISS BELL: I did meet him three months before the murder, and again the day before.

BROWN's COUNSEL: What is your relationship to the prisoner George Richardson?

MISS BELL: I don't know what you mean.

BROWN's COUNSEL: I suggest to you that you are his mistress and are giving evidence to help him.

MISS BELL: That's a bloody lie.

JUDGE: Miss Bell, you must behave yourself. If you speak like that again, I shall deal with you for contempt of Court.

MISS BELL (half crying): But I'm a respectable girl, I am—and it's wicked things to say of me.

JUDGE: If that is true, I can understand your feeling upset, but you must control yourself in Court.

MISS BELL: I'm sorry, my Lord.

BROWN'S COUNSEL: Do you swear that you have never stayed the night with George Richardson?

MISS BELL: I certainly do.

BROWN'S COUNSEL: I suggest to you that that last answer is quite untrue. Are you not his mistress?

MISS BELL: May I be struck dead if I am.

BROWN'S COUNSEL: Now would you mind answering the question?

The case goes on and eventually the jury return their verdict on the charge of murder in the case of all three men. It is Guilty. All three men lodge appeals against the conviction. But Brown's counsel is at first hard put to it to find grounds for the appeal. There was ample evidence against his client. In the witness box he had to admit that he did take part in the warehouse-breaking. He said he must have picked up the watchman's cap instead of his own by mistake, when running away from the scene. He said that he saw the watchman lying on the ground. He had already been struck. He had no idea that violence was going to be used. He did not know which of the others had used it. He did not go for help as he was frightened. He did not know whether the man was dead or injured. Miss Bell's story was utterly untrue.

D

The judge's summing up was absolutely fair. But, as Brown's counsel was trying to make up his mind what grounds of appeal he could put in, his solicitor came to him with some urgent information. In consequence, when the appeal came on for hearing before the Court of Criminal Appeal, Mr Spooner, Brown's counsel, had more to say than he had originally thought possible. Grant and Richardson were less fortunate; the jury had obviously thought that they were parties to the crime even if they had not struck the blow themselves. The summing up was unassailable. Their appeals were dismissed. But the case of Brown was rather different.

BROWN'S COUNSEL: Your Lordships will observe that there is only one ground for this application. I have most carefully considered every aspect of the matter and I am satisfied that I could not properly urge your Lordships that there was any misdirection by the learned judge or that the verdict was against the weight of the evidence. I am applying to your Lordships for leave to call further evidence but, before I do so, I desire to remind your Lordships of the salient features of the case.

Mr Spooner then outlined the main evidence given at the trial.

BROWN'S COUNSEL: I respectfully submit, my Lords, that this was essentially a case where everything depended upon the jury's view of the evidence of the witnesses.

VERNON J.: Apparently they did not believe your client.

BROWN'S COUNSEL: I quite agree, my Lord. They did

not. I go further. I say that they probably believed Miss Bell. If, however, they had disbelieved Miss Bell they might well have had some doubt about the guilt of my client. He had behaved most foolishly no doubt. But the lies he told the police were quite consistent with his being innocent of murder. The same applies to his and his wife's original story about the cap. His behaviour throughout, in my respectful submission, was the behaviour of a frightened man, but not necessarily that of a man guilty of murder. He had admittedly been engaged in committing a felony, he had seen the night watchman dead or badly injured, he might well have been terrified. I agree, my Lord, that it does not speak well for a man to have to admit that he left another man who might have been alive without going to his help. But my client is not convicted of callousness or extreme fright but of murder. Now, my Lords, Miss Bell swore that she was not the mistress of the prisoner Richardson and, furthermore, as far as the jury could tell, she was a woman of good character. The only thing one could say against her was that, having been told that a crime, possibly involving violence, was going to take place, she did not go to the police. Her explanation was that she thought the appellant was just boasting. She did not believe for a moment there was anything in it. She thought that he probably read strip cartoons and certain crime books which made him think it was a clever thing to say.

VERNON J.: I'm sure you made that criticism of her evidence very ably to the jury, Mr Spooner.

BROWN's COUNSEL: I did my best, my Lord, but, my Lords, I did nothing to what even I could have done

if I had had the evidence which I now seek to tender
to your Lordships.

VERNON J.: What is the nature of the evidence?

BROWN'S COUNSEL: My Lords, in the first instance
I have a witness who will say that the lady was the
mistress of George Richardson and, for reasons which
I think will satisfy the Court, that witness was not
available to the defence at the trial. Secondly, I have,
through the assistance of the Director of Public Prosecutions, ascertained that Miss Bell had some years
previously been convicted under another name of
making a false statutory declaration.

VERNON J.: What are you asking us to do?

BROWN'S COUNSEL: To hear this evidence.

VERNON J.: All of it?

BROWN'S COUNSEL: Yes, my Lord.

VERNON J.: Your client, as you must know but the
jury did not know, has a pretty bad record himself,
has he not?

BROWN'S COUNSEL: I agree, my Lord.

VERNON J.: Many convictions for breaking and en-
tering and one for violence—*to avoid arrest*.

BROWN'S COUNSEL: That is so, my Lord.

VERNON J.: Now, for my part, I agree that in a case
of this kind the conviction for making a false statutory
declaration—which in effect is a conviction for perjury—might have been a very important factor in the
case. I agree that the evidence of Miss Bell may well have
had some influence on the jury when they considered
your client's case. I agree that, if you had had before
them the material you seek to tender now, they might
well have taken a different view of Miss Bell's evidence.

But what about your client, Mr Spooner? What about his evidence? If Miss Bell had had her conviction put to her, your client could have had all his convictions put to him. As it was, the jury had no idea that your client had a bad character or that he had had a conviction for violence against him.

BROWN'S COUNSEL: It might well have left the jury in some doubt, my Lord, but then they would have acquitted the appellant.

VERNON J.: How can this Court say what the jury would have done? If all that evidence had been given both for and against your client, a different verdict might have been returned. I don't know. This Court can't re-try the case, you know.

BROWN'S COUNSEL: If your Lordships will hear the evidence——

VERNON J.: What then? Are we to hear the appellant cross-examined as to his previous convictions as well?

BROWN'S COUNSEL: I am content that your Lordships should take those into account in determining the matter.

VERNON J.: But we are not the jury, Mr Spooner. They are the tribunal to take such matters into account. It seems to me, on what you have so far stated, that this is eminently a case where the appellant ought to be tried again by a fresh jury. That's what ought to happen if real justice is to be done in this case. But, unfortunately, this Court has no power to make that order. I can only express the hope that it will not be long before Parliament gives us that power. Meantime, we must consider how to deal with this case.

So the argument proceeds as to whether the other

evidence should be admitted or not. Counsel for the
Crown agrees that Miss Bell had the conviction referred to, but, of course, the prosecution were unaware
of it at the time of the trial or they would have informed Brown's advisers. With regard to the other
evidence, counsel can only say that Miss Bell still
denies that she was Richardson's mistress. Eventually,
after full argument, the presiding judge gives the
Court's decision.

VERNON J.: If we did what we have been pressed to
do, we should in effect be re-trying the case and
usurping the province of the jury. How can we say
what the jury would have decided if all the evidence
had been in front of them? They might still have convicted, though they might have acquitted. This Court
has a duty to the public—as well as to the appellant.
In our considered view, justice requires that this man
should be re-tried, but we have no power to re-try him
or to order him to be re-tried before a jury. Our
jurisdiction is limited to quashing a conviction or
dismissing an appeal. It is true that we have power to
hear further evidence but, in our view, we cannot adopt
that course when to do so would in effect be to put
ourselves in the position of the jury. In the present case
it would be for the jury to weigh up the bad record of
the accused against the one conviction of Miss Bell, and
to consider the evidence of a person who apparently
will swear that Miss Bell was Richardson's mistress
against her own oath that she was not. In the result
the appeal of this man will have to be dismissed,
although, if he were re-tried, as he ought to be, he
might have been convicted or acquitted. No doubt the

proper authority will consider what should be done in the matter.

In other words, the Home Secretary will have to consider what should be done about it. But he cannot order a new trial. All he can do is to make such enquiries as he thinks fit. He may take the course of appointing a well-known lawyer to hold an enquiry in private. But what could such a lawyer do? No doubt he could form his own conclusion as to whether Miss Bell was Richardson's mistress or not. But the jury might have formed a different conclusion. And, as for Miss Bell's conviction, what can the Home Secretary or any lawyer or any person or persons except another jury do about that? Probably, in a case like this, the Home Secretary would advise commutation of the sentence to imprisonment for life. It was possible that Brown was innocent altogether of murder but, because of the absence of power to order a new trial, the best that can be done for him is to commute his sentence.

That is an example of a case where the lack of power to order a new trial works against the interests of an accused person. Now, here is a different type of case. In Brixton Prison, Thomas Hugg is being interviewed by his counsel. He has been committed for trial on charges of robbery with violence. He is in fact guilty, but he asserts his innocence to his counsel and relies on a thin alibi.

HUGG: Well, what d'you think of it? Have I got a chance?

COUNSEL: Everyone has a chance until the jury say he's guilty.

HUGG: What'll I get if I go down?

COUNSEL: A lot. It's a bad case if you're guilty.

HUGG: Yes—but how much? Ten years?

COUNSEL: Probably.

HUGG: If you get me out of this, I'll go straight for the rest of my life.

At that stage counsel could not get him out of it. The jury convicted him, and the judge gave him the expected ten years. But, a day or two later, he saw his counsel at Wormwood Scrubs Prison on the question of an appeal. At first Thomas Hugg was not very pleased at his counsel's apparent cheerfulness.

HUGG: It's all very well for you to look like a ray of sunshine . . . what about me? Ten years. And for a first offence.

COUNSEL: First offence?

HUGG: Well, they've never got me before.

COUNSEL: Anyway, never mind about that. I've some good news for you. The judge made a bad mistake in his summing up—it was just a slip, of course, but I think you'll get away with it in the Court of Criminal Appeal.

HUGG: D'you really think I've got a chance?

COUNSEL: It's always dangerous to prophesy, but I think you've got a jolly good one.

HUGG: If you get me out of this, I'll go straight for the rest of my life.

In due course the appeal comes before the Court of Criminal Appeal, and Hugg's counsel proves not to have been too optimistic. The presiding judge gives the decision of the Court.

JUDGE: This appeal must be allowed. We feel bound to say that we quash the conviction with the greatest regret. There was ample evidence against the appellant and the crime was a wicked and cowardly one, resulting in an old man being seriously injured. Undoubtedly, however, the learned judge misdirected the jury on a point which we cannot say was of no material importance. We have been urged by counsel for the Crown to say that, in spite of the mistake, there has been no miscarriage of justice, but, although none of us has much doubt that, if the jury had been properly directed, they would have returned the same verdict, we cannot say that this must inevitably have happened. What ought to happen in the interests of justice is that the appellant should be re-tried before a fresh jury, but we have no power to make that order, and we have no alternative but to quash the conviction and order the immediate discharge of the appellant.

Extract from the daily Press twelve months later:

Last night an elderly woman was found badly injured outside a shop in the West End. Robbery was apparently the motive.

That was Thomas Hugg's latest victim. If he had had a new trial she might not have suffered pain for the rest of her life.

On the other hand, a most distinguished lawyer in a Debate in the House of Commons on the 1st July 1960 deplored the suggestion that there should be power to order a new trial. 'If you are fortunate enough to be set at liberty,' he is reported in *The Times* (2nd July 1960) as saying, 'let it be final and nobody thereafter should challenge the order you might have been lucky to obtain.' Very nice for the Huggs of this world but not so pleasant for the elderly women whom they rob.

Now, of course, the facts were contrived in both the fictitious cases just related to lend support to the argument in favour of the power to order a new trial being given to the Court, but neither of them was in the least an exaggeration, and a case of each type could easily occur and very likely has occurred or will occur. In other words, there are cases where either appellants or the public are worse off by reason of the lack of power to order a new trial.

Admittedly it is far more often that the public are worse off. The question is: Should they be? Which is the worse, that people like Hugg should go free to commit further crimes or that people who are probably guilty should have the unpleasantness of undergoing two trials, and the witnesses have the inconvenience and (it may be) expense of giving evidence twice, and the public bear the bulk of the cost? If the second trial would not be fair there could only be one answer to this question, but, if the suggestion already made were adopted, it would not be ordered unless it would be fair or the appellant preferred to have it.

4   *Magistrates' Courts*

MOST of the criminal work in this country is decided by non-lawyers. Although all the more serious cases are tried before a judge and jury, there are far more less serious than serious cases and the vast majority of these are decided by justices of the peace. In London and some of the big cities there are professional legally qualified magistrates, but all the rest of the Magistrates' Courts are presided over by justices. They are advised by their clerk (who is in most cases a qualified lawyer) but the decision is theirs and not the clerk's. No doubt they will usually accept his advice on matters of law but on questions of fact and on the amount of the penalty they should act entirely on their own discretion. Practically every case, serious or not very serious, starts in the Magistrates' Court, and nearly all the less serious cases end there. In most cases, where a sentence of imprisonment exceeding three months can be imposed, a man has a right to trial by jury, but in the majority of these he does not exercise that right and elects to be tried by the magistrate or magistrates. Apart from motoring offences, the usual criminal cases tried by magistrates consist of some form of stealing or obtaining money by false pretences. But they also deal with separation and maintenance orders between husband and wife and affiliation orders and certain other matters such as non-payment of rates.

59

Justices of the peace are unpaid, but the Metropolitan and stipendiary magistrates are, of course, paid. From time to time complaints are made in the Press about the different penalties which are inflicted at different courts. It is inevitable that, whether the Court is presided over by lay magistrates or a professional magistrate, there must be divergencies of opinion as to the proper penalty to award. And no one who was not present in Court, or who has not a shorthand record of the proceedings, can properly criticise any penalty imposed. For example, the man may have had previous convictions not mentioned in the report. But unquestionably from time to time a man will get what the public considers too light a penalty in one case and too heavy in another. But this would happen even if all the magistrates were legally qualified. It happens now with judges. But it is true to say that usually the decision of judges and legally qualified magistrates are between certain not-too-far-apart limits.

One judge, however, might well give a man two years, and another judge give him three. One Metropolitan magistrate might send a man to prison for a month, and another fine him or put him on probation. If a judge errs in principle, the Court of Criminal Appeal will alter the sentence imposed. And there is always an appeal available from a magistrate to Quarter Sessions, who will have a complete discretion about the sentence.

It is quite right that decisions of judges or magistrates which appear to the public to be wrong—to be too severe or too lenient—should be criticised in the Press. But it is absurd to suggest that, because this happens, there is something wrong with the system. It is possible that, if all Magistrates' Courts were presided over by qualified lawyers, there would be less wide discrepancies, but there might be disadvantages outweighing that possible advantage.

In England there are about 200 judges and legally qualified magistrates; in Germany before the war there were about 5,000. There would have to be a vast increase in the number of stipendiaries if the system of using justices of the peace were abolished. Apart from the cost which this would entail, the standard of justice would in all probability be very much lower than it is at present. It is most unlikely that there are a sufficient number of practising barristers and solicitors (there are certainly not enough barristers[1]) capable of doing the work satisfactorily who would be prepared to take it on at the sort of salary which would be offered. As a tribunal a bench of laymen advised on matters of law by a solicitor is infinitely preferable to a third-rate lawyer sitting by himself. It is, however, fair to add that it is only recently that solicitors have become eligible for appointment as legally qualified magistrates, but it is difficult to think that, if the Bar cannot produce sufficient numbers of efficient magistrates prepared to do the work at present done by justices of the peace at the salary which would be offered, solicitors would be ready and able to supply the deficiency in numbers.

The present system works extremely well on the whole, but, of course, mistakes are made from time to time and are, quite rightly, criticised. But, just because

[1] There are only about 2,000 practising barristers in England and Wales altogether.

in a ten-line report of one case a man is stated to have been sent to prison for six months for stealing a bottle of milk, and in a similar report of another case a man is fined £5 for obtaining £20 by false pretences, this does not mean that the system is a bad one. And, even if it were desirable, on the whole, to replace laymen by legally qualified magistrates, there are other defects in the administration of the law upon which the money could be far better spent, and one of them is concerned with the Magistrates' Courts in London.

These are mostly presided over by lawyers, although, owing to the amount of work, certain courts have justices of the peace to assist as well. A vast amount of work is dealt with in these courts, far too much in fact, and it speaks extraordinarily well for the efficiency and good temper of the magistrates that no serious complaints are heard about the way in which justice is administered in these courts. But the fact is that cases are tried, and have to be tried, at far too fast a rate; the length of time between the issue of a summons and the hearing of a case is often far too long; and there are far too many adjournments. Anyone who has the slightest doubt about this should spend a couple of days in one of these courts. The speed at which the magistrates work is fantastic, and, although they discharge their duties admirably, it is utterly wrong that they should be compelled to work so fast. If they worked slower their lists would get into even more disorder, delays would be even greater and there would be even more adjournments. A person's recollection of an accident may not be good a few minutes afterwards. What is it likely to be some months later? By that time the witness is more likely to be reciting some excerpts from his imagination than to be relating what he really saw.

A motoring charge may not be of great importance to the public, but it may be of considerable importance to the person concerned, and no one ought to be hurried in the trial of such a case. Even if it is only a case of obstruction by a motor car, a person may be sent to prison for non-payment of any fine inflicted, and it is absolutely wrong that he should get the impression that the Court is in a hurry. It is quite true that no magistrate increases the fine because the defendant has taken up a lot of time by pleading 'not guilty' and talking a lot, but any defendant could be excused for thinking that that was likely to happen to him. Few, if any, Metropolitan magistrates would dispute that they are compelled to work at a ridiculously fast pace.

Now without money there is nothing the authorities concerned can do about it. It would be useless to appoint more magistrates at the moment because there is nowhere to house them. What is required are more courts and more magistrates, and without them both the present system will continue. And the danger is that, the longer the present system goes on, the greater the grip the present method of administration of justice in these courts will get on the magistrates and their clerks. If a speed of a hundred miles an hour is maintained for many years it will appear to be the right speed, and all calculations of the number of courts and magistrates required will be based upon that speed being the proper speed. Unless, therefore, something is done soon to remedy the present situation there is a real danger that the present speed will become traditional.

These are the only courts where this speed is maintained. In every other court, High Court, County Court, Quarter Sessions, when a case does come on for trial, there is no atmosphere of hurry, and the litigant is not made to feel that he must get it over as soon as possible and make way for the next case. And it must be remembered that the magistrates are dealing mostly with cases where a man's liberty or character or, at the least, his motoring character is involved. Or they may be dealing with matrimonial disputes which are often of vital importance to the parties.

If it seems astonishing that the public and Parliament have not decided that something drastic must be done about it, and that the building of new courts must start at once, it must, of course, be remembered that it is easy for anyone who has not the responsibility of using the money to say that this or that must be given priority. It may be that no priority can be given to the building of Magistrates' Courts and an increase in the number of magistrates. If that is so, however, the country is very unfortunate, for the need is great and the present situation is gravely unsatisfactory. Hospitals and homes must no doubt come first. But should large blocks of offices? The Government could, if the country could afford the expense, find ample building materials and labour for making additional courts.

5 *Costs in Criminal Cases*

THE question whether an accused person who is acquitted is to be paid his legal costs has caused a good deal of controversy recently. It is not in the least an easy question and it involves the consideration of a number of matters.

Before a person can be convicted of crime in this country his guilt must be proved beyond all reasonable doubt. The fact that he is acquitted does not mean that he is necessarily innocent. It only means that his guilt has not been sufficiently proved. An employee might be prosecuted for stealing and be acquitted. He could then bring a civil action against his employer for wrongful dismissal, false imprisonment or malicious prosecution or all three. In that action his employers could raise the defence that he was in fact guilty of stealing. And although the man had been acquitted at the Old Bailey, a judge or jury in the Queen's Bench Division might say that he was guilty, for the measure of proof in the civil action for wrongful dismissal is not so high as at the trial for stealing.

In the Queen's Bench Division the employer only has to prove that there was a preponderance of probability that the man stole. So a man can be acquitted by a Criminal Court and 'convicted' civilly. In such a case he could not be fined or sent to prison. He would simply lose his civil claim and have his character prejudicially affected. The fact that this cannot have happened on more than a very few occasions is probably due to two reasons: one is that most acquitted persons are satisfied not to have been convicted and would not dream of taking any civil proceedings; they are quite happy with their luck up to date. Secondly it may also be partly due to the fact that until recently it was not appreciated that a man's guilt does not have to be proved beyond all reasonable doubt in a civil court but only by a preponderance of probability. Until 1956 it was thought that the measure of proof in both courts was the same. Hence, if a criminal prosecution had failed, few people were prepared to try to prove guilt again if it had to be so conclusively proved.

Most people who have had wide experience of the Criminal Courts would agree that only a very, very small percentage of innocent men are tried for serious offences. Many people are acquitted—and quite rightly —because their guilt is not sufficiently proved. But this does not mean that they were innocent. In the Magistrates' Courts, where lesser offences are tried, there is rather more room for error than in the cases which are sent for trial by jury. In the latter cases there have not only been police enquiries but a full enquiry before a magistrate as well. In the lesser cases which are tried before a magistrate, the prisoner may have been arrested the day before the hearing and, although there are often adjournments for further enquiries to be made, there is more room for error. Even so, in the vast majority of cases tried before a magistrate the accused persons are guilty, though again and for the same reason a substantial proportion are acquitted.

English lawyers and the English public recoil at the idea of an innocent person being convicted and accordingly the scales are weighted heavily in favour of those who are accused of crime. There is also a strong feeling that, if a man is acquitted, however lucky he may have been, he should be entitled to treat the verdict as though it meant that he was innocent. The Scottish verdict of 'not proven', which leaves a slur on the accused's reputation, would not be acceptable to the English public, who believe that it must be one thing or the other.

So, unless an acquitted person is foolish enough to stir up things again by bringing an action for false imprisonment or malicious prosecution or the like—in which case he might today find to his horror that a civil judge or jury said he was guilty—he is to be treated as though he were completely innocent.

Who, then, is to pay the costs of his defence? Obviously, if, although acquitted, he has behaved in such a manner as to justify his prosecution, it may well be that he ought not to have his costs. For example, a man who breaks into somebody's house to sleep and opens cupboards and drawers out of inquisitiveness, but not with any intention of stealing, can hardly complain if he is charged with breaking in with intent to commit a felony. On the other hand, a man whose main defence is an alibi, and who claims that he must have been mistaken for someone else, ought to have his costs—if he is acquitted. It may be that the alibi is a flimsy one, but, if it causes enough doubt of his guilt in the minds of

the jury to make them acquit him, the judge's disbelief
in the genuineness of his defence should have no effect
on the order as to costs. It is the jury's view that should
count.

But there is another aspect of this matter which
receives far too little consideration by the public. In
some cases a man's defence is that the witnesses for the
prosecution are mistaken. In those cases a verdict of not
guilty does not reflect upon those witnesses. But in other
cases the defence is that the witnesses are committing
perjury. In such cases a verdict of not guilty, if understood to mean that the accused is innocent (not simply
that his guilt has not been sufficiently proved), can
reflect gravely upon the witnesses and, it may be, with
gross unfairness. The witness has had no trial, no
opportunity of employing counsel to represent his
interests, or to do anything except answer the questions
he has been asked. The prisoner is acquitted, newspapers announce 'John Jones cleared', and people start
saying that the witnesses ought to be prosecuted for
perjury, or dismissed the police force, or as the case may
be. Yet the truth may be that the jury very nearly
convicted the prisoner but were not absolutely satisfied.
They may have infinitely preferred the evidence of the
prosecution witnesses to that of the accused, but have
felt some slight doubt.

Not long ago, in a case of an alleged sexual assault,
the woman who was the chief witness for the prosecution
committed suicide after the trial. The defence of the
accused was consent and he was acquitted. No one but
the parties knew exactly what the truth was, but,
suppose the corroboration of the woman's story was

insufficient to satisfy the jury of the guilt of the accused, it rightly acquitted him but did not necessarily mean to imply anything against the character of the woman. But who was to tell her that? The jury could have added a rider that it did not disbelieve the woman, but simply felt it unsafe to convict on the evidence. This would have been equivalent to a verdict of 'not proven', and would to some extent have smeared the character of the person acquitted.

Everyone always concentrates upon the man in the dock, and few people give so much as a thought for the witnesses for the prosecution. They may, of course, not be vitally or in any way affected by the verdict, whatever it is, but, on the other hand, they may be gravely affected by it.

It can, therefore, be seen that a verdict of not guilty may cause great injustice, but how is it to be avoided? It is certainly not for the judge to express his own personal views, though in a proper case he might think fit to say something for the benefit of a witness. But in many cases it would be almost impossible for him to say anything in favour of a witness without at the same time casting a slur on the accused, quite or almost as much as if the jury added a rider doing so. No jury has ever returned a verdict of 'Not guilty but lucky'.

It will now be seen that the question of costs can, in some cases, be tied up with this other problem of injustice to someone who was not in the dock. To take an example: in a police prosecution for assault, where the defence is an alibi and where the possibility of mistake by the policeman concerned can be ruled out, how is a verdict of not guilty to be construed by the judge? If he awards costs against the police, that might appear a strong pointer to the guilt of the police, but the jury might in fact have preferred the police evidence and have given its verdict by reason of the absence of corroboration.

What is the solution? If it is the right view that, if a person is acquitted (however luckily) he should be treated (as far as the criminal law is concerned) as innocent, then it would prevent an inference unfair to anyone being made if, as a matter of right, every acquitted person had the costs of the defence paid for out of public funds, except in one or possibly two cases. If a man's admitted conduct fully justified the prosecution—in other words, if it was not, for example, a case of mistaken identity but a case where the accused had on his own admission told lies or was guilty of other wrong conduct leading to his prosecution—in such a case the judge should have power to deprive the acquitted person of all or part of the costs. Such a provision would be fair to the public and to the man. Secondly, it might be that the jury should have power to express a view that a man should not be given his costs. But the objection to this exception is that it is a little like the verdict of 'not proven'. And, equally, the failure of a jury to make such a recommendation could always be used by some people to suggest that the jury was satisfied that the witnesses for the prosecution were lying. Otherwise, it would be argued, it would have recommended that the accused had no costs.

On the whole, it would appear that the award or deprivation of costs should not fall within the province of the jury, and in a sense the fairest rule would be that costs were automatically given to the accused unless his admitted conduct constrained the judge to deprive him of all or part of the costs. That would cast no *unfair* slur on the acquitted person, as the reason for the deprivation would have been his *admitted* conduct. In other words, although he was to be treated as innocent of the crime itself he admitted doing or saying things (not amounting to the crime) which were either very foolish or very reprehensible.

When it is suggested that this is 'in a sense' the fairest rule, it is certainly not absolutely fair, inasmuch as at least nine out of ten people who would benefit by it would in fact have been guilty of the crime of which they had been acquitted. But, for reasons which have already been dealt with, this type of injustice is one which most people prefer to accept, as it is the chief method of avoiding what is considered an intolerable injustice, the conviction of an innocent person.

But even if the suggestion made is a desirable solution, it cannot be adopted unless the public can afford it. The solution to some injustices can only be arrived at by the expenditure of public money, and, as there must be some limit to the drain on the public purse, it becomes in each case a question of priorities. Which is the more important—that crime should be reduced by increasing the pay of the police force or that acquitted prisoners should be paid their costs of being defended? If the public can afford both, so much the better, but, if only one, which is the more important?

6 *Other Criminal Problems*

THERE are some other aspects of crime which require consideration. If a man is charged with a crime and found 'guilty of the act charged but so insane at the time as not to be responsible therefor' (a verdict commonly referred to as 'guilty but insane'), he has no right of appeal to the Court of Criminal Appeal. This seems to require remedying, and one argument alone seems incontrovertible. In such a case the man's main defence may be that he did not do the act charged against him, but his relatives and friends or legal advisers may have persuaded him to rely alternatively on the defence of insanity. Why should such a man be deprived of the right of the ordinary convicted person to appeal against the verdict that he did the act charged? Evidence may have been wrongly admitted, the judge may have badly misdirected the jury on the facts or law relating to the crime, or there may be vital further evidence not available to the accused at the trial which he would like to bring before the Court of Criminal Appeal. If he is found 'guilty but insane' he cannot do any of these things. His main defence may be an alibi but it makes no difference. However many mistakes are made by the prosecution and the judge, and however assailable the summing up, he cannot appeal.

It seems impossible to bring forward any fair or logical argument for depriving the accused of the right of appeal as far as the facts are concerned. But at the moment he has none. Presumably the reason that the law has not yet been amended is because no case has yet arisen in this country which patently showed the need for the change. In most if not all cases where insanity is in issue the accused is not challenging the facts, except insofar as a state of mind is a fact. He admits he pulled the trigger or used the knife or certainly does not deny it. Indeed he rarely goes into the witness box. But one day such a case will arise and it would surely be better to alter an obvious defect in the law before the need arises. It is quite true that the Home Secretary may have sufficient power in some cases to deal with what would otherwise be an injustice, but it would be more dignified of the law not to have to rely on this outside remedy to put right its defects.

Some little disquiet may be caused to the public by the recent book on the Podola trial and some reviews of it. It has been suggested that if a man, although fit to stand his trial, has lost his memory of the facts relating to the crime, he should not be tried but detained until his memory has returned. The jury found that Podola had not lost his memory but, suppose they had found that he had, ought he to have been tried or not?

A little consideration of the matter suggests most strongly that such a man should be tried. Of course, if he asked for a reasonably short adjournment to see if he recovered his memory, no doubt the application would be granted, but that is not suggested. The proposition is that a man who has genuinely lost his memory should be treated as a man unfit to plead and detained indefinitely or until his memory returns.

Now what is the reason for this proposition being put forward? It is because an accused person who has completely forgotten the facts relating to the alleged crime is at a grave disadvantage in conducting his defence. So he is, unquestionably. But he is able to understand all that is happening at his trial, to instruct solicitors and counsel and to call witnesses. Now in many criminal trials a man may suffer from a grave disadvantage. A man charged with manslaughter on the road may have been struck on the head himself and rendered unconscious, and he may never remember anything of the accident. Is he never to be tried? A man similarly charged who is uninjured himself may have had a person sitting next to him who could have corroborated his story but for the fact that that person was so injured and remembers nothing. A bystander may have been so shocked or injured by the accident— or indeed later on at another accident before the trial —that his memory of the facts relating to the accident has gone. In many ways the loss of a witness in this way is a far greater disadvantage than an accused's own loss of memory, particularly if it were an independent witness in another car or a bystander. Although the evidence of an independent witness *may* be completely valueless in a civil trial, there is no doubt that such a witness's evidence favourable to an accused on a criminal trial would be of great value. No one, however, suggests that, because a *witness* other than the accused has lost his memory, a trial should be indefinitely adjourned.

There are all sorts of disadvantages, grave and less grave, from which a person in the dock may suffer, but they cannot be reasons for more than a temporary adjournment of the trial, and loss of his own memory is no more and no less than a grave disadvantage. Witnesses for the prosecution may still be cross-examined to show that they are liars or mistaken.

Indeed it may in fact be a great help to an accused person to have lost his memory, whereas, if a witness he was proposing to call to give evidence dies or goes insane or disappears, it may be an appalling disadvantage.

In every case where the accused suffers from some such disadvantage the prosecution and the judge will help him, as far as they properly can, to overcome the disadvantage, but more cannot surely be expected. It may be a disadvantage that Mr A appears for the prosecution and Mr B for the defence. It would be greatly to the benefit of the accused if it were the other way round. The judge may be Mr Justice X whereas Mr Justice Y is generally believed to be a more satisfactory judge from the prisoner's point of view. Unknown to the prisoner and his advisers there may be on the jury a highly intelligent and determined man who has a rooted objection to the particular method of killing which the accused is alleged to have adopted, and the rest of the jury may have little power of resistance. These disadvantages have to be accepted without question. So has the absence of witnesses or *their* loss of memory.

Justice in human affairs cannot be perfect, and those who take part in its administration can only do their best. Once the principle that a trial cannot go on at all if the accused is at a grave disadvantage for any reason at all (except that he is of unsound mind) is accepted, the principle could be applied for one reason or another in a host of cases.

It is true that, unless there were a fixed penalty of death or imprisonment for life, the accused would prefer to go on with the trial with all its disadvantages, but, if it would be wrong in principle to go on with the trial where the prisoner did not want it to go on, it would be wrong in principle to go on when he preferred it to go on. If this were the law, most men found dead drunk in the street and charged with being drunk and incapable could probably never be tried. In many cases they would have to admit that they remembered nothing, and they would be detained until their memories returned. This would never happen in fact, though, if that were the law, one can visualise an accused person giving a detailed (though entirely fictitious) account of all he had drunk and all he had done the previous evening. When a man thinks he is going to be imprisoned for life it brings back his memory wonderfully, as Dr Johnson might have said.

A suggestion has recently been made by a high sheriff who was very much impressed by the way in which criminal trials are conducted. During his period of office he was present at a large number of such trials and admired the fairness which was shown to the accused throughout. The one matter which he thought could be improved upon was the method of sentencing a man. Then he felt that the prisoner, standing pretty well numb in mind and body waiting for sentence, was incapable of taking in the words used by the judge in passing sentence other than the actual sentence itself. He has made the suggestion that a copy of the judge's remarks should be given to each prisoner later on. This is no doubt an excellent idea and may well be adopted in due course, but there are occasions when perhaps as a matter of discretion it would be better to leave matters as they are.

For example there is a type of prisoner who would not be best pleased or derive much benefit from reading in the quietness of his cell:

'You are a very wicked man and I can find no redeeming feature whatever in your case.'

To be allowed to keep this sort of remark as a souvenir is a privilege which might not always be appreciated. And, indeed, a prisoner, charged with striking a warder in prison, might plead as his defence that the warder handed him this:

'The public must be protected from men like you.'

He could accept the sentence but didn't see why it should be rubbed in after the proceedings were over.

On the other hand, of course, some old hands might prize such remarks.

'Look at this, guv. "The worst case of its kind I have ever tried." That was old 'Alliday, guv. And 'ere's a nice one. "You grow older but no better." But that wasn't 'is own, guv. I read that one years before 'e said it. 'Ere, and what d'you say to this? "A pest to society." But this is the one I like best. "I don't know what to do with you. You've never done an honest day's

work in your life, except when you've been in prison."
They know something, these old judges. Quite right
the old basket was. Always 'ave 'ated work. 'Ow d'you
think 'e knew, guv?'

Then again one might find this sort of thing:

'I can quite understand the excuses you have put
forward. You were in a position of great temptation and
your needs were greater still. I accept your story
entirely. In a sense it may be said that you were more
sinned against than sinning and I hope that, when you
come out of prison, you will be able to lead a happy and
useful life. Meanwhile it is my unpleasant duty to pass
a sentence upon you of ten years' imprisonment.'

At least the man concerned would have plenty of
time to read and re-read it.

7 *Judge-made Law*

THE benefits of the Common Law of England (largely judge-made law) are almost universally recognised. In this country it has enabled the law in many cases gradually to change in accordance with the changed habits of society, without the necessity for Acts of Parliament. This saves expense and delay and relieves Parliament of business for which it could ill afford the time.

But this does not mean to say that the Common Law system is perfect or that it could not be improved upon. Its main defects are the cost of remedying judges' mistakes and the injustices which may take place until those mistakes are corrected.

'My Lord,' said counsel once, 'it surely won't hurt for the evidence to be given? There's no jury to be prejudiced.'

'No,' said the judge, 'there isn't. But there's me.'

Bad grammar but good sense. Although professional judges can be trusted never to be absurdly swayed by sentiment or prejudice, they are in fact human and unquestionably wrong decisions occur as a result of judges, even of the highest distinction, being prejudiced. The usual prejudice is in favour of someone's merits, though it may be against someone's demerits, but in either case an attempt is made to trim the law and the facts of the particular case so as to produce what seems to the judge in question a just and fair decision in the matter before him.

The fact that this decision may result in subsequent injustice does not always sufficiently occur to him. His motive is, of course, an excellent one, and most members of the public seeing him at work on the particular case would applaud him as an admirable and fair-minded judge. They could not be expected to see ahead, but the judge can be so expected, and it is because he is prejudiced that he does not. And the odd thing is that, if he had realised the effect that his decision was going to have on subsequent cases, he might have been even more prejudiced the other way.

Here is a good example of a real case which eventually went to the House of Lords.

Mr and Mrs White were one day walking along the road wondering how to solve their immediate diffi-culties. They had bought a house on mortgage but, after paying the deposit and a number of instalments, they found that the cost was more than they could afford. As soon as they became in arrears with the instalments, like sensible and honest people they decided to do something about it. First of all they ascertained that their house was worth at least £2,300 and that a sale at this price would leave them sufficient for their own purposes after the whole of the mortgage debt had been repaid. The problem, therefore, was to find a small flat which they could afford. This was no easy matter, but, as they were walking along, they stopped outside an estate agent's office and were delighted to see advertised just the sort of flat they wanted at just the sort of rent they could pay.

Wondering why it had not already been snapped up, they went into the office and found to their delight that it was still available. They asked if they could see it. Before answering their question, the representative said:

'Have you a house to sell?'

'As a matter of fact we have.'

'Very well then, I'll take you to see the flat.'

Mr and Mrs White must have become quite excited, because they knew that the flat was protected by the Rent Restriction Acts, that the very modest rent could not be increased except by the amount of any increase in the rates, and that no premium could be charged. It was a piece of luck they had hardly dared to hope for. And there was more good news for them still. When they saw the flat they found that it would suit them admirably. So they said at once that they would take it.

'Just a moment,' said the representative, 'how much d'you want for your house?'

They said: '£2,300–£2,400.' They had already described the house to him.

'Very well,' said the representative, 'you can have the flat, but only if you sell your house for £1,800.'

'£1,800! But that's £500 less than it's worth.'

'I know,' said the representative, 'but, if you want the flat, that's how it's got to be.'

Mr and Mrs White worked out with the agent what would be left to them on this basis, and asked if, in the circumstances, a little more could be allowed to them.

'No,' said the representative, 'it's £1,800 or no flat.'

Mr and Mrs White thought it over and finally decided to accept the proposition. They had nowhere

F

else to go. They could just repay the mortgage debt
with £1,800 and have a little over, and they felt they
had no alternative. So they sold their house for £1,800,
and got the flat.

Now the purchaser of the Whites' house was a limited
company (Company A) and the landlord of the flat
was another limited company (Company B), and it
may be wondered why Company B, who got nothing
out of the transaction, wanted to be so generous for the
benefit of Company A. An examination of the Share
Register of both companies disclosed the reason. One
family had the bulk of the shares in each company. In
other words, the family concerned was, in effect, getting
an illegal premium in respect of the letting but hoped
that, as they were only getting it by reason of their
share-holdings, the transaction would be held to be legal.

Eight distinguished judges, three in the Court of
Appeal and five in the House of Lords, held that this
sale at an undervalue to Company A was as much
payment of a premium as if £500 had been paid to
Company B and they ordered Company B to disgorge
the £500. It may well be asked why such a plain case of
an attempt to drive a coach and horses through the
Rent Restriction Acts should have taken up the time of
the Court of Appeal and the House of Lords, and
involved so much legal expenditure. It was due to an
earlier but erroneous statement of law by one of the
most distinguished judges of the century, the then
Lord Chief Justice.

He had the keenest sense of justice and a deep anxiety
that right should prevail, and his reputation as a lawyer
was as high as any judge's in any court, and higher than

most. It is, therefore, almost inconceivable that his view of the Whites' case would have been different from the view of all the judges in the Court of Appeal and the House of Lords.

But the merits of the tenants in the earlier case were not so conspicuous as those of the Whites. It was a case where the prospective tenants of flats which were being made out of converted houses in Birmingham paid sums to the builders concerned. The landlords of the flats were held by the Birmingham Rent Tribunal to have required an illegal premium to be paid to the builders. The Lord Chief Justice delivered the judgment of the Court, which decided that the payments were not illegal premiums, and that, for a premium to be illegal, it must be paid to the landlord. The money was paid to the builders and, therefore, the Court mistakenly decided, no offence was committed and the money could not be recovered by the tenants.

This statement of the law in the Birmingham case was expressly overruled by the Court of Appeal in the Whites' case, and the only reason that the Whites' case went to the House of Lords was because the Whites' landlords hoped that the House of Lords would reverse the Court of Appeal's decision and uphold the Lord Chief Justice's statement in the Birmingham case. But their persistence was not rewarded and they had to bear the costs of all the proceedings from start to finish. It was, however, a mere chance that the Birmingham case was decided by a Court whose decisions were not binding on the Court of Appeal. But, had the Birmingham decision been a decision of the Court of Appeal, as it might easily have been, the Whites would have lost their case in the Court of Appeal (which ordinarily has to follow its own previous decisions) and, unless they had been able to appeal to the House of Lords, they would have suffered a serious injustice.

Now the strong probability is that, but for the decision in the Birmingham case, the Whites' case would not have gone beyond the County Court. The Birmingham decision was binding there and the County Court judge, contrary to his own view, felt bound to follow it. Otherwise he would have decided in favour of the Whites.

The Birmingham case was a comparatively innocuous one where it presumably appeared wrong to the Court which decided it that the landlords in that case had been guilty of a criminal offence. And they so construed the law as to acquit them. Whether that decision gave the idea to the landlords in the Whites' case is not known, but it is as certain as anything can be that, had the Whites' case come first, the decision in the Birmingham case would have been the other way round.

What happens is this. Someone's merits or demerits persuade a court to give a wrong decision. As judges are human, this is quite unavoidable. But the result of the mistake is not limited to the parties to the one case, and the cost of correcting the mistake may be very considerable and has to be paid by someone. By whom should it be paid?

Fortunately, in the Whites' case, all the costs were paid by the people who had tried to devise the ingenious scheme for defeating the Rent Acts, so that in that case justice was substantially done. Not entirely, because, although the Whites were legally aided, there were certain costs which had to be paid out of their contributions to the Legal Aid Fund. This aspect of the matter will be dealt with further in the chapter on Costs in Civil Cases.

But the fact that justice was substantially done in that case was an accident. The people who had to pay a very large sum to get a wrong decision put right might have had all the merits. Considerable injustice results from wrong decisions. For years people may pay money which is not legally due from them, because of such decisions. For example, for about seven years a decision of the Court of Appeal[1] enabled an estate agent to get commission, or the equivalent of commission, from his client even if the house was never sold, e.g. where the client changed his mind about selling it. Then eventually the House of Lords reversed this decision and from then until very recently there was a series of decisions, nearly all against the estate agent. Indeed to such an extent did the Courts appear to have been 'prejudiced' against estate agents that, not long ago, a High Court judge, in deciding against an estate agent, said that he was constrained to do so 'by the philosophy of the decisions' of the Courts. Two judges in the Court of Appeal objected to this phrase, although one reserved his view on that matter. All four judges, however, decided against the agent.[2]

[1] *Trollope v. Martin* 1934 2K.B. 436.
[2] Although it is not strictly within the ambit of this book, it may be worth pointing out to estate agents that if there is or has been any prejudice by the Courts against them, it is probably because the judges concerned thought it unreasonable that a houseowner should have to pay full-scale commission even if his house was not sold. They may have felt that the owner of a house should not be compelled to sell his house in order to earn commission for an agent and that the owner

Recently, however, there has been a decision[1] of the Court of Appeal in favour of estate agents, and it was held that the agreement made by the owner of a house compelled him to pay commission even though he withdrew the house from the proposed sale. The decision appears to be correct, but it is highly desirable that the House of Lords should pronounce upon it. Otherwise it is conceivable that exactly the same will happen as happened after *Trollope v. Martin*. Since this new decision owners of property will be well advised to get legal advice before they sign an estate agent's agreement which contains anything more than simple instructions to sell.

It is obviously unsatisfactory that, where a mistake has been made by a judge or judges, the entire cost of remedying that mistake should fall on a private individual or company. It should fall on the public. This possibility of the costs of successful appeals being paid for out of public funds is considered later. But it might also be possible to devise a scheme to keep the Common Law in better order.

For example, it could be provided that, whenever a decision affecting a substantial number of members of the public appeared to be unsatisfactory, it could be

---

ought to be allowed to change his mind at any time before a binding contract has been made with a proposed purchaser of substance.

It is, however, well-known that, although an agent may earn a commission by doing very little, he may do a great deal of work and get nothing. The Courts would have no objection whatever to some reasonable clause being inserted in the agreement between the agent and the client to provide for reasonable remuneration and expenses being paid to the agent if the client changed his mind after a willing and able proposed purchaser at the agreed price had been introduced.

[1] *Drewery v. Ware-Lane* 1960 3A.E.R. 529.

brought to the attention of the Law Officers, who should have the duty of causing a hypothetical case on the subject to be argued in the Courts. As a result, either the decision would be over-ruled or, if found to be legally correct, Parliament could, if it chose, pass legislation to deal with the matter. In this way a continuous watch would be kept on doubtful decisions, and it would not be left to private people to pay for public mistakes.

It would involve some expense, but the Law Officers could be assisted by a small committee of first-class lawyers, who could sift the cases before any proceedings were taken. It would be open to anyone to call the committee's attention to any cases of apparent mistakes or uncertainties. It would be for the committee to say first whether a sufficient number of people were affected by the decision in question to justify public expense.

Trollope v. Martin is a good example, for the decision in that case which enabled the agents to get money to which they were not entitled was only a majority decision. It was dissented from by a well-known judge, Lord Justice Scrutton, and it was an obvious case affecting a large section of the public which could have been put right if the system suggested had then existed. *Drewery v. Ware-Lane* is not a doubtful decision but it will have far-reaching effects, as some agents may now adopt the clause used by the agents in that case and many unsuspecting members of the public may agree to it. It is highly desirable that the construction of the clause should be pronounced upon by the House of Lords.

The Courts have always resisted attempts to obtain

decisions from them on purely theoretical points. They will only try real cases, and a test case must be a genuine one, not a pretended one. But, apart from the question of expense, there could be no real objection to points of law being decided for the public benefit, provided the initiation of such proceedings was properly controlled.

The case of the Whites was a real case where, in fact, very little harm was done, but the next chapter contains a description of a fictitious case which could affect almost everyone in the country. And one day someone may have to pay a lot of money to put the matter right. What happens if, without your fault, water or gas escapes from your house or flat, shop or business premises, on to your neighbour's property and does him harm? One might have thought that the law was clear on the subject. It is not.

8   *Little Drops of Water*

SLEEPING as comfortably as Mrs Brown's elbow in his back allowed him, Mr Brown was dreaming of running brooks. He was in the country by a rivulet which was flowing past him from high ground. He listened happily to the sound. It was a soothing one. As he listened, the countryside receded into the distance and his bedroom in Elphinstone Court started to appear. He realised that he was awake but, for a moment, continued to listen happily to the running water. Then in a flash he appreciated that what may sound lovely in the country is wrong altogether in the bedroom of an upper flat in London.

He jumped out of bed and into the bathroom. Water was pouring from the lavatory cistern. He turned off the tap, woke up his wife and with her wondered how much damage had been done in the flat below. The seed of litigation had been sown.

The first question the Browns had to consider was whether to disturb their neighbours below, the Blacks, in the middle of the night. Their relationship had not been of the best up to date.

'Whatever we do will be wrong,' said Mr Brown. 'If we wait till the morning they'll say a lot of extra damage has been done. If we call them now they'll say we've woken the baby and why couldn't we have kept it till the morning.'

'I can't stand that woman,' said Mrs Brown. 'She always seems to sniff when we pass them.'

They stood discussing the matter for a few minutes. They were an important few minutes. Whether or not Mr Brown was liable for what had happened so far, he would become liable for what happened thereafter, if he did not act as a reasonable man, and so might Mrs Brown if she did not act as a reasonable woman. It is not surprising that complaints are made at the law which expects people to be reasonable when they've been woken up at 2.30 a.m. by a faulty cistern. But so it is. This matter of reasonableness will be considered in a separate chapter.

Mr and Mrs Brown eventually decided that, however unpleasant the consequences, they must wake up the Blacks, and Mr Brown took the unhappy duty on himself. He knocked several times on the Blacks' door before a sleepy Mr Black asked him what the devil he wanted at that time of night. For a moment Mr Brown felt like going upstairs again—saying something like: 'All right, if you don't want my help, go without.' But better sense prevailed and he explained what had happened. The effect on Mr Black was electrical.

'Your bathroom!' he exploded. 'It's partly above my study, isn't it?' And, before Mr Brown could answer, he rushed away—almost tripping over his dressing-gown in the process. A moment or two later Mr Brown, who, not having been invited in, was still standing at the door, heard shouts of anger mingled with oaths not usually heard in Elphinstone Court. By this time Mrs Black was up and she joined her husband. 'Look!' Mr

Brown heard him scream. 'Look at that! Look at it! They're ruined. Ruined.'

A moment later the Blacks' baby woke up and joined in the general protest.

'Is there anything I can do?' asked Mr Brown as loudly as he decently could.

The sound of Mr Brown's voice reminded Mr Black that the cause of the disaster was at hand. He rushed to the door.

'D'you know what you've done?' he shouted.

'I'm very sorry,' said Mr Brown.

'Sorry!' exclaimed Mr Black. 'Sorry! What's the good of that? They're ruined. Absolutely ruined.'

'Might I know what?' asked Mr Brown.

'My stamp collection. I had them all out last night, and hadn't put them away, as I hadn't finished with them. Your blasted water has ruined the lot.'

'I'm terribly sorry,' repeated Mr Brown.

'So you said,' said Mr Black, a note of grimness in his voice. 'But nothing like as sorry as I am—or as you're going to be. This is going to cost you a lot of money, Mr Brown. D'you know what my collection is worth?'

'I'm afraid I've no idea.'

'Well, if you had, you might have taken a little more care to keep your water to yourself. It was worth over a thousand pounds.'

'I'm very sorry,' said Mr Brown, 'but I don't really think it's our fault. The ball must have been suddenly broken away from the arm.'

'And whose cistern is it, may I ask? Am I responsible for keeping your cistern in proper order? You'll hear from my solicitors about this. Good night.' And Mr Black slammed the door.

Mr Brown returned to his wife, who had heard everything.

'Oh, dear,' she said, 'what horrid people. Has he really got a stamp collection, d'you think?'

'It sounded like it,' said Mr Brown.

'But will we really have to pay for it?'

'Heaven knows,' said Mr Brown. 'We'll need a lawyer, as well as a plumber, to sort this one out.'

In the morning Mr Brown sent for the plumber and Mr Black went to his solicitor.

The plumber confirmed Mr Brown's diagnosis of the cause of the accident.

'It's broken off,' he said.

'Yes,' said Mr Brown, 'but why?'

'Because it couldn't stick on no longer.'

'How long do they usually last?'

'A month. Twenty years. Any time.'

'What can you do to prevent this sort of thing happening?'

' 'Ave an earth closet, mister. Nothing else that I knows of.'

'You mean that the ball may break off at any time from the moment you buy the thing, and there's nothing you can do to make sure it won't?'

'That's right, mister. It don't often happen, but you can't never tell when it's going to. Like as not it'll last the life of the cistern. Done much damage?'

'Well, I don't really know, but my neighbour downstairs says it's ruined his stamp collection.'

'I expect 'e's insured.'

'Oh, I hadn't thought of that. Let's hope he is.'

Now Mr Black was insured and, when Mr Brown discovered the fact, he was at first delighted. But his pleasure did not last long, for it was in fact Mr Black's insurance company's solicitors who eventually wrote to Mr Brown making a claim for over £600. This sent Mr and Mrs Brown off to a solicitor and within a day of receiving the claim they were interviewing Mr Glewbody of Groaner and Glewbody.

After they had shown Mr Glewbody the solicitor's letter, and explained what had happened, Mr Glewbody got up and took a book from a shelf.

It was a volume of Halsbury's *Laws of England* (3rd edition).

'Let me see,' he said, as he looked at the volume. 'The first question is whether you were guilty of negligence. If what your plumber says is right, I don't think you were. But, of course, another plumber might say that there ought to be periodical inspections of these cisterns.'

'And suppose he does?'

'Well, then it'll be for the judge to say which view he accepts.'

'What's he likely to say?'

'That will depend entirely how they give their evidence and on the result of cross-examination. But, if we take several opinions, we ought to be able to find out what the general view is on the subject. Personally, I've never known of a ball becoming loose before, but then I'm not an expert.'

'Well, suppose the general view is that there was

nothing we could have done to prevent the accident, are we all right?'

'That's just what I'm looking to see,' said Mr Glewbody. 'My recollection is that, although the general rule is that if you bring water on to your premises you are absolutely liable if it escapes, this doesn't apply to ordinary domestic water.'

'Then we're all right on that point?'

'I'm just looking. Ah—yes, here we are. Rickards and Lothian. Yes, that's right. You are not responsible if ordinary domestic water escapes without any negligence on your part.'

'Good. Then it's just a case of whether we can find enough plumbers to support our case.'

'Yes, I think so,' said Mr Glewbody. 'But just a moment. What's this?'

He stopped for a moment as he read a paragraph.

'Who came to the premises first, you or the Blacks?'

'Oh, they were there a long time before us. They've been tenants of what was the top floor for years. Then we bought the house and added a floor above.'

'I see,' said Mr Glewbody. 'And did Mr Black agree to your adding a floor?'

'Like hell he did,' said Mr Brown. 'I beg your pardon. No, he did not. He fought us every inch of the way, but we got permission from the local authority in the end.'

'I see,' said Mr Glewbody. 'That makes it rather awkward.'

'Why?'

'Well, the cases seem to say that the reason you're not liable for the escape of domestic water is because the person below expressly or impliedly consents to your keeping a supply above them.'

'But I thought you said there was a case which said that ordinary domestic user was all right?'

'Yes,' said Mr Glewbody, 'I did. But these later cases seem to say something else.'

'Seems rather like the plumbers to me,' said Mr Brown. 'Does it depend on how many cases you find on each side?'

'Not exactly,' said Mr Glewbody, 'but I think perhaps this is a case where you'd be well advised to consult counsel.'

'What'll that cost?'

'Ten guineas or so. It's no use going to anyone inexperienced. You must go to a good man.'

'And suppose we're in the right? Will we get the money back?'

'I doubt it.'

'That seems very unfair. Black's insurance company threatens us with proceedings if we don't pay the claim. If we're in the right why shouldn't they pay the cost of our taking legal advice?'

'You must address that remark to your Member of Parliament, Mr Brown. All I can say about it, I'm afraid, is that I shall require a cheque from you to cover counsel's fees.'

So this is the first injustice encountered by the Browns, and the problem of legal costs is difficult of solution. The provisions of the Legal Aid and Advice Act have not lessened the problem and it will be discussed separately in the chapter on Costs in Civil Cases.

Mr and Mrs Brown were not eligible for assistance under the Legal Aid and Advice Act, and so they went off with Mr Glewbody to see counsel. Mr Greenacre, the barrister whom Mr Glewbody usually briefed, was a cheerful man of reasonable ability and he enjoyed his profession enormously. He particularly liked finding interesting points of law, and to his surprise Mr Brown's case provided him with one.

'I'm most grateful to you,' he said, shortly after he had been introduced to his clients. 'I believe the Court of Appeal has gone wrong.'

Mr and Mrs Brown received this piece of information without particular enthusiasm.

'It may be necessary to go to the House of Lords to put them right.'

'Who is going to the House of Lords?' asked Mr Brown. 'I've always heard it's expensive.'

'Yes,' said Mr Greenacre cheerfully, 'I'm afraid it is, but on the whole I don't think you'll have to go there.'

'That's a comfort.'

'Though one can never be sure. Have you ever heard the story of the famous silk a good many years ago? There had been tremendous litigation between two large companies culminating in a protracted hearing in the House of Lords, which ended in a compromise. One of the companies gave a dinner to all concerned on its side and the famous silk was one of the guests. He was invited to speak, and this is what he said: "As a general rule I never speak unless I'm paid but, on this occasion, I'll give you three words of advice free. Litigate, litigate, litigate." And he sat down. As the lawyers were the people who had gained most out of the case the cold reception given to this speech was not unreasonable.'

'Quite,' said Mr Brown, 'but I should like to make it plain that I view any kind of litigation with distaste, and I don't propose to indulge in it unless I can be assured of a reasonable certainty of success. I should prefer to pay £600 rather than risk losing £6,000.'

'Absolutely,' said Mr Greenacre. 'I should feel the same in your position. And I may tell you that, oddly enough, lawyers in this country do not as a whole create or encourage litigation. They try to prevent it from being started and to bring it to an end by a compromise once it is started.'

'Then how do they live?'

'Fortunately many litigants will not accept their advice and those cases, combined with the cases which for one reason or another cannot be compromised, keep us alive.'

Mr Greenacre's statement is substantially true. There are, of course, exceptions to the rule, but the average solicitor or barrister acts almost every day to his own personal disadvantage in the manner described by Mr Greenacre.

But even though Mr Greenacre had no intention of deliberately trying to involve the Browns in dangerous and expensive litigation, it was very difficult for him to advise them correctly without doing so, and the reason is this.

In the second half of the nineteenth century the House of Lords decided, in a case called *Rylands v. Fletcher*,[1] that if a man brought water or any other

[1] (1868) L.R. 3H.L. 330.

G

'mischievous' substance artificially on to his land he was absolutely liable if it escaped and damaged someone else's property, except perhaps in the case of an Act of God. Later decisions laid down that an Act of God or the King's enemies, or the malicious act of a third person over whom the occupier had no control, should exempt him from liability. That meant that, however careful he might be, whatever the cause of the escape (with the exceptions mentioned) he was responsible for the damage caused by the escape. The principle adopted was that, if he chose to bring water on to his land to make an artificial lake or a swimming pool or for some other purpose, he must ensure that it hurt no one. And, after all, he need not bring it on to his land. If he chose to do so for his own purposes, and it escaped, he must take the consequences.

But problems soon began to arise about domestic water—baths, lavatories and so on. Suppose the water escaped below, was the occupier of the flat from which the water escaped liable for damage it caused, however careful he may have been? Various judges, not always quite for the same reason, said 'No', and, in 1913, the Privy Council[1] said in terms that the bringing of water on to domestic premises was not only usual but more often than not required by the local authority. Rightly or wrongly, they held that the decision in *Rylands v. Fletcher* was based on the fact that it was an unusual use of land to bring water artificially on to it, but they held that it was not unusual use of land in the twentieth century to bring water on to it for ordinary domestic use.

[1] *Rickards v. Lothian* 1913 A.C. 263.

If matters had rested there all would have been well, but unfortunately they did not. In 1943 a case[1] arose where a sprinkler system had been installed in a theatre in case of fire. Without any fault by anyone there was an escape of water which damaged goods in a warehouse underneath the theatre. Now this was not a 'domestic' use of water, and, therefore, the cases covering domestic water did not on the face of them apply. On the other hand, undoubtedly water had artificially been brought on to land. Now the object in this case was a very good one. The theatrical proprietors installed the water to save lives. It was not at all like a case of a person installing a swimming pool or some other such luxury. There was no negligence on the part of the theatre employees and no judge can be blamed for wanting to say that, in the circumstances, there was no liability on a careful person who had brought water on to his land for such an excellent purpose. It may well be that just as domestic water became a normal use of land, so sprinkler systems in theatres and similar places became in the twentieth century a normal use of land and, on that basis, the case could have been satisfactorily decided in favour of the theatre. But the Court was not satisfied to do this. Reviewing all the earlier cases the Court of Appeal (reversing the decision of the judge below) came to the conclusion that the basis upon which the owner of domestic water in the flat above is not liable for escape of water in default of negligence is that the person underneath has impliedly consented to his keeping the water upstairs. In other words, the Court said that

[1] *Peters v. Prince of Wales Theatre (Birmingham) Ltd.* 1943 1K.B. 73.

when a man takes a flat he knows there's a bath and lavatory above him and, by taking the flat below, he accepts the risk of accidental flooding from above.

So the Court virtually discarded the reason given by the Privy Council and stated that *consent* was the real basis upon which the domestic water cases were to be distinguished from *Rylands v. Fletcher*. Having reached that conclusion the Court held that there was also consent in the theatre case and, as consent was the only thing that mattered, the fact that it was not domestic water did not matter and the theatre proprietors were acquitted of all liability.

This case was followed with approval in a subsequent case in the Court of Appeal,[1] and in the result a number of distinguished judges have said that the correct basis of the domestic water cases was consent. It may well be that the same conclusions as were reached in all these three cases could have been reached without laying down this doctrine, but the fact is that the doctrine was laid down.

What then of Mr Brown's case? In that case, so far from Mr Black consenting to Mr Brown having a flat with domestic water erected over him, he hotly contested it. In no way did he consent to water being laid on above him. If, therefore, the true basis of the domestic water cases is consent, Mr Brown was presumably absolutely liable for escape of water. On the other hand, no one has ever sought to say that the judges in the Privy Council case were wrong in saying that the principle is that the provision of ordinary domestic water is not an unusual use of land. If that is

[1] *Prosser v. Levy* 1955 3A.E.R. 577.

the correct view, the Browns are not liable in the absence of negligence by them. But, if consent is required, they are liable. Yet it seems very hard on the Browns. They were given the necessary permission by the authorities concerned to erect their floor, they owned the whole of the building and the Blacks were only tenants. Why should the Browns' position be any different from any other occupiers of a flat?

But what would appear to have happened is that, in order to find a satisfactory ground for giving effect to the merits of the theatre proprietors, the Court laid down a wrong principle which will only be appreciated when the case of Brown *v.* Black really arises.

Disregarding almost entirely the grounds given by the judges in the Privy Council case for their decision, the Court of Appeal has expressly or impliedly held that, where houses are next door to each other and are entirely independent of each other, the occupiers are apparently absolutely liable for the escape of water, or gas, sewage or the like unless the escape is due to the Act of God, the King's enemies or the malicious act of a person for whom the occupier is not responsible. They can be as careful as they like but if there is an escape for any reason but the exceptional ones mentioned, they must pay.

Now the reasons laid down by the judges in the Privy Council case for relieving the occupier of liability in default of negligence would equally apply to adjoining houses as to flats one above the other. What the Privy Council said in effect was that in modern times the provision of water, gas, electricity and drainage systems were essential to ordinary standards of living and that, when that involved the bringing on to the land of mischievous substances, the occupier was under no liability for escape if he took all reasonable steps to avoid it. The judges only referred specifically to gas and water but it is plain that the same principle applies to electricity and drainage systems. They said that the principle of *Rylands v. Fletcher* did not apply where there was 'ordinary use of land or such a use as is proper for the general benefit of the community'. They further said: 'The provision of a proper water supply to the various parts of a house is not only reasonable but has become in accordance with modern sanitary views an almost necessary feature of town life. It is recognised as being so desirable in the interests of the community that in some form or other it is usually made obligatory in civilised countries. Such a supply cannot be installed without causing some concurrent degree of leakage or overflow. It would be unreasonable for the law to regard those who instal or maintain such a system of supply as doing so at their own peril. . . . He is only using the premises in an ordinary and proper manner.'

It will be seen that that statement of the law has nothing whatever to do with consent, and provides a good, sensible code of conduct required from the occupier of a building whether used for business or domestic purposes. But unfortunately the decisions of the Privy Council, although regarded in all courts with the greatest respect (with certain exceptions immaterial to this case), are not absolutely binding on any English court, whereas those of the Court of Appeal are. That Court has laid down a basis for its decisions which may result in litigation going to the House of Lords at someone's expense or alternatively in unjust decisions.

The strong probability is that in the end the law will be held to be that laid down by the Privy Council and the basis of the Court of Appeal decisions will be held to be wrong, but if that is not the case, legislation will be necessary to remove a defect in the law. This is a situation which may arise any day between adjoining owners whether of houses, flats or business premises. The Court of Appeal indeed distinguished between the cases of neighbouring independent houses and those of flats or premises in the same building. On the other hand, the principle of the decision of the Privy Council is equally applicable to neighbouring houses as it is to flats.

What is the law? At the moment one will have to wait until the case of Black and Brown arises and goes as far as the Court of Appeal or House of Lords.

If the country could afford it, it would certainly be a step towards preventing injustices, if problems such as this one could be decided by the Court *before* they arise. But if this is considered a luxury which the country cannot at present afford, it is no good complaining at the injustice when it arises. If you can't afford the cure, you must accept the illness philosophically.

A somewhat similar problem arises when Mr Justice A gives judgment for the plaintiff and the Court of Appeal reverses the judgment and gives judgment for the defendant. Or when Mr Justice B gives judgment for the defendant and the Court of Appeal reverses his decision and gives judgment for the plaintiff. In

each of these cases the parties have both acted reasonably. In the first case the plaintiff must have had a
reasonable case or the judge would not have found in
his favour. Similarly, in the second the defendant must
have had a reasonable case or the judge wouldn't have
found in *his* favour. All the additional costs were caused
by the judge in each case making a mistake. Or, if you
took the case one stage further and the House of Lords
reversed the Court of Appeal's decision, the expense
would have been caused by the Court of Appeal
making a mistake. If three judges decide in a man's
favour he must usually have a pretty reasonable case,
even if he is eventually found to be wrong. Is it justice
that he should have to pay so much for the judges'
mistakes? But, if he does not pay, then who is to do so?
Not the judges themselves, though no doubt this would
give great satisfaction to some disappointed litigants,
and even to some of their legal advisers. But it is obvious
that to make a judge liable for such costs would in a
way make him an interested party in the litigation.
In order to arrive at what he considers a just decision a
judge must not be subject to pressure of any kind. The
only people left to pay, if it is not to be the litigants
themselves, are the public at large.

The public has to pay for so much that it may well
be that at present the costs of other people's litigation
is not a fair additional burden. Litigation may be said
in some cases to be a luxury. Why should the public be
responsible? It already bears a share under the Legal
Aid and Advice Act.

On the other hand the administration of justice is
very important, and it is also very important that every

person should feel that the Courts are open to him—not like the Ritz Hotel but like a hospital—without risking crippling expense.

It would not be impossible to devise a scheme which, subject to proper safeguards to avoid frivolous appeals and the like, would provide that in the case of appeals where a judge's decision is shown to be wrong the State should pay the costs of both sides to the appeal in any event, unless the Court in its discretion saw fit to order one or other or both sides to pay them because of unreasonable conduct of some kind. After all, the State appoints the judges and, if the judges cause expense by making mistakes, it is not unreasonable that the State which chose the judges should pay for the mistakes. Moreover, some of these mistakes may have been due to the difficulty of construing Acts of Parliament. For example, Parliament certainly bears a heavy responsibility for the costs involved in interpreting the Rent Restriction Acts.

How much money the adoption of the above suggestion would involve could be ascertained approximately, and the public and Parliament could then consider whether the claims of justice had sufficient priority over other claims to justify such a new departure.

It may well be thought by some people who have read this chapter and the previous one that the system of judge-made law is a bad one. Why not scrap the lot and simply have codification as they do in France, for example? Theoretically (but only theoretically) this is, of course, right, but the answer to this criticism is that it has been found beyond the wit of men to codify laws so that they provide for every particular case. The result is that there are just as many decisions in France not expressly provided for by the Code Napoléon as there are decisions in England. But there is this difference. No judge is bound by the decision of another judge in France and, though he may in fact follow a precedent, he is not bound to do so. In consequence there is even less certainty in France than there is here. Moreover the English system is a flexible one, and as the country's mode of living changes so, within certain limitations, can the law recognise the change. The case in the Privy Council provides a good example of this, the judges recognising in effect that it was no longer an unusual use of land to bring piped water on to it for certain purposes. In the seventeenth century a domestic supply of water would most likely have been held to be unusual and mischievous.

There is accordingly no method by which absolute justice can be obtained, and, as far as one can tell, unless we can learn a new and perfect system from some inhabited planet, never will be. But our own system can be substantially improved in certain aspects, if, and only if, the public is prepared to pay for the improvement.

9   *Accidents*

ANY reader who has been involved in a road accident or has been near to one knows that whatever did happen happened in a very short space of time, at the most in a few seconds, and sometimes in less than a second. There are not many people who, in these circumstances, can say with certainty and honesty what really did happen. It is, of course, a stock legal joke that immediately before an accident both the cars concerned were stationary, so that they could not have collided with each other—although they did. This has been improved upon because, in one recent accident case, according to one of the parties, both cars were going backwards.

What most people do not perhaps realise is that in many of these cases it is almost, if not quite, impossible to ascertain with any certainty at all what happened and to whom the blame should be attributed or how it should be apportioned. Yet judges are attempting this task every day.

A few years ago an experienced judge stated in his judgment that, while one or other of the parties to the accident must have driven abominably he was quite unable to say which of them was at fault. He said that he was quite unable to say that the one case was more probable than the other.

Now any judge could, if he chose, say 'I accept the evidence of Mr A,' when he did not really know whether to accept Mr A's or Mr B's evidence. In the case in question the trial judge could have tossed up for it and then pretended to accept the story of the plaintiff or the defendant—according to the way in which the coin fell. But that is not the way in which judges are expected to arrive at their conclusions, and, as they are people of integrity, if they say they have come to a conclusion, that is because they can put their hands on their hearts and say with sincerity that they have. Some cases may be on the border-line, and it is only after considerable thought that the judge has come to a conclusion at all—and it may be that he still has some misgivings, which he mentions when he pronounces judgment—but eventually he is able to say that by a preponderance of probability (and that is all that is required) he has come to a particular conclusion.

But it is surely possible that in a particular case, especially one relating to a road accident, a judge might find a respectable plaintiff, a respectable defendant, no other witnesses, no marks on the road and nothing beyond the word of the parties to help him come to a conclusion. Cross-examination leaves both parties unscathed. For example:

PLAINTIFF: I was driving slowly on the proper side of the road when the defendant in passing a dark saloon car coming towards me came over the white line and struck my wing.

DEFENDANT'S COUNSEL (cross-examining): I suggest to you that exactly the opposite occurred, and that you tried to pass a car on your side of the road, crossed the white line and struck my client's car.

PLAINTIFF: Certainly not. There was no other car going on my side of the road.

PLAINTIFF'S COUNSEL: Perhaps my learned friend will state the number of the car which my client is supposed to have passed?

DEFENDANT'S COUNSEL: We haven't got it, any more than you have the number of the car my client is supposed to have passed.

PLAINTIFF'S COUNSEL: At least my client gave some description of it.

DEFENDANT'S COUNSEL: I'm obliged to my friend. I'd like a little more description. You say my client passed a dark saloon car. How many doors had it?

PLAINTIFF: I don't remember. It was gone in a second.

DEFENDANT'S COUNSEL: What was its actual colour? Black, dark brown, dark green or what?

PLAINTIFF: I tell you it was gone in a second. I just got the impression of a dark car.

DEFENDANT'S COUNSEL: You only got an impression, did you? Perhaps it was an illusion.

PLAINTIFF: It was nothing of the kind. Your client's car passed it.

DEFENDANT'S COUNSEL: Then how did you see it if my client's car was passing it?

PLAINTIFF: I saw it before your client passed it. It was the first car I saw. Then your client overtook it.

DEFENDANT'S COUNSEL: If you saw it for so long, how is it you can't remember the colour?

PLAINTIFF: I wasn't taking any particular notice of it until your client started to pass it, and then there was the accident and the other car was gone.

And so the cross-examination proceeds, with the plaintiff sticking to his story. After that the defendant goes into the witness box, gives his version in much the same way and is cross-examined similarly.

Some people think that judges can penetrate the hearts and minds of men. They certainly sometimes appear to do so, because the truth has a nasty habit of coming out. But in such a case, where the plaintiff and the defendant are equal in character and in their demeanour in the witness box, what is a judge to say? There is also the difficulty that in many of these cases by the time the witnesses have come to Court they really believe their evidence to be true. Some undoubtedly always believe themselves in the right from the start and, even if they are hopelessly in the wrong, start to invent for themselves (if for no one else at that stage) a story in their own favour almost before the accident. By the time they give their statement to a police officer or to their insurance company it is a wonder that the driver about whom they are speaking has not been prosecuted for dangerous driving. But with many drivers the process is slower, though it is none the less certain. The advantage of the process being slower—that is to say, the advantage from the point of view of a judge trying the case—is that some drivers may make statements to the police immediately after the accident which are completely at variance with their subsequent evidence. That does not mean that they are committing perjury because, by the time they go into the witness box, they are quite convinced in their own minds that their evidence is true. But in such cases the evidence of the police officers to whom the original statement was made is a great help to the judge in his effort to find out which is the more probable story.

No lawyer would dispute that in coming to a conclusion about an accident case a judge may well be wrong. Not long ago two judges tried cases arising out of the same accident. One judge came to one conclusion, the other to a completely different conclusion. The Court of Appeal restored order by reversing the decision of one of them. But not every case goes to appeal. Also, not long ago, a jury awarded a boy very heavy damages for terribly severe injuries. The judge entered judgment for the boy. He must, therefore, have felt that there was evidence on which the jury could properly have given their verdict. The Court of Appeal by a majority of two to one set aside the verdict, and held that there was no evidence to justify the finding of the jury. Thus two Supreme Court judges and a jury have held that the boy should have damages, and two Supreme Court judges have held that he should not. The result? The boy gets no damages—unless the House of Lords should reverse the Court of Appeal decision.

One only has to think of the various possibilities in an accident case to see how difficult it is to have any assurance that a just decision will be given. All judges do their best to give a just decision but their task is often impossible and the cases just quoted substantiate this.

A man is knocked down by a vehicle and badly injured. What are the possibilities relating to a claim by him for damages?

1. He may not have seen what happened.
2. He may have seen what happened but have been rendered unconscious and forgotten it.
3. There may have been an independent person standing near the scene of the accident.
4. That person may have seen the accident or
5. he may not.
6. If it has actually passed in front of his eyes his brain may not have taken it in; he was thinking of football pools and not particularly looking at the traffic.
7. He is an intelligent man capable of telling an articulate story or
8. he is not very articulate.
9. He makes a statement to a police officer in which he and the officer misunderstand each other.
10. He makes statements to insurance companies, solicitor's clerks and his wife.
11. He is a good witness and is not particularly nervous nor rattled by counsel or
12. he is a bad witness.
13. He makes a mistake in his evidence and goes to pieces as a result of cross-examination.
14. The driver of the car had a passenger or
15. he hadn't.
16. He makes a good statement to a police officer or
17. a bad one.

This could go on for ever and furthermore there is an

infinite variety of ways in which the plaintiff's or the
defendant's or an independent witness's evidence can
be very well given or very badly given, and, in either
case, it may be quite inaccurate. At the end of it all the
judge has to give judgment, saying whether the man is
entitled to damages in respect of an injury which may
have affected him for life. The judge knows that usually
an insurance company will find the damages if the
plaintiff wins. No judge would be human if he did not,
in those circumstances, *want* to find for the plaintiff.
There have been cases in the past where judges went
further than that and allowed their sympathies to
weigh as much with them as juries are supposed to do.
But although this has happened, and although a judge
might prefer to decide in favour of a badly injured
plaintiff, he normally decides the case to the best of his
ability one way or the other, however sorry he may be
for the injured plaintiff.

There are now five to six thousand people killed a
year and hundreds of thousands injured on the roads.
The public as a whole is responsible for these deaths
and injuries, inasmuch as everyone makes use of motor
transport in one way or another. Even a bedridden
person uses motor transport, as many of his needs are
brought to his home or the hospital where he lies by
such transport. When someone is killed or injured by
one of these lethal weapons (which everyone is directly
or indirectly using) is it satisfactory that the decision
whether or not damages are to be awarded in respect
of such death or injury is to depend upon so many
uncertainties? It is in many cases a complete gamble
whether damages are to be recovered or not. The

gamble depends on the presence or absence of witnesses and their reliability, and on the ability of the judge who tries the case to come to a correct conclusion. In these circumstances what are the chances that justice will be done in any particular case?

Accidents which only involve material damage are far less important. It is quite true that cases about them are just as difficult of solution as cases of personal injury, but if a mistake is made no one is going to be ruined by it. If a man's leg has to be cut off as the result of a road accident, it is surely just that the public as a whole should compensate him for the loss of his leg, even if he was wholly or partly to blame himself—unless, of course, he was trying to commit suicide or, for other reasons, deliberately tried to have an accident.

Apart from these last cases (which would be very rare and which could be excepted from the general rule) would it not be more satisfactory that any person injured in a road accident should obtain fair compensation from public funds? The premiums already paid to insurance companies would partly provide the means from which to do this, and the rest could be obtained by increasing the amount payable by way of national insurance. Apart from the quite exceptional cases referred to, no one deliberately gets involved in an accident and the fact that everyone was automatically insured against the consequences of an accident would be unlikely to make people more careless. No one would give his life or even a leg for £20,000.

The amount to be paid as compensation could be fixed, as it is now, by a judge, or in the same way as industrial insurance claims are now handled. Probably a judge's decision would be better but, once the principle of national insurance against death or injury on the road was established, there would be no difficulty in fixing the method of computing the damages.

It may be said that there are just as many accidents in the home as on the roads. But in those cases the public as a whole is not responsible. And, furthermore, it is far easier to fix the blame. But the public, having decided to accept the killing of several thousand people a year on the roads, and the injury of hundreds of thousands, in return for the benefit it gets from road transport, ought to foot the bill for these deaths and injuries and not leave it in a great measure to chance as to whether the bill is to be paid at all.

Such national insurance might deprive the legal profession of a good deal of litigation, though there would still be the necessity to fix the damages. But, contrary to popular belief, lawyers do not strive to make business for themselves, and there was no outcry among them when workmen's compensation was abolished and industrial assurance took its place. If lawyers were satisfied that national insurance was a fairer way of dealing with claims for death and personal injury on the roads, they would certainly be ready to adopt the same attitude as they did towards workmen's compensation.

There is one further matter relating to accidents which is not a question of law at all. Everyone wants accidents to be reduced, but no one has yet produced any constructive suggestion to reduce them within any reasonable space of time. All kinds of suggestions are made for increasing penalties, removing licences and so forth. But general legislation can have no appreciable effect, if it will have any at all. In the first place, there are nothing like the number of police required to detect and prosecute more than a tiny proportion of those who commit offences on the roads. Secondly, juries are very chary of convicting motorists. If a man is convicted by a jury of driving while under the influence of drink he must be very drunk indeed. It will be remembered that under the original Act of Parliament a man had to be 'drunk' before he could be convicted. This was altered because the Court said 'drunk' meant 'drunk', and merely being under the influence of drink was not the same thing. But Parliament might have saved itself time and trouble. The words might be 'dead drunk' as far as juries are concerned. And even then they might say to themselves: 'The poor fellow was very tired, that's why he was lying in the back seat trying to steer with his feet. Not Guilty.'

Moreover, many accidents are caused entirely through the fault of pedestrians, pedal cyclists, the parents of children and the owners of animals. Penal legislation would not make them any more careful.

What is required is to make every member of the community realise that if everyone (including pedestrians, cyclists, motorists, children and parents of children) took a little extra care the accident rate would drop heavily. No one wants these accidents and, if it were conclusively proved to the public that a little extra care would avoid them, there is at least a chance that the standard of everyone would improve.

Now there is a method by which this could be done.

The cost would be trifling compared with the benefit to be gained, it would involve no legislation and would not alter the normal daily life of anyone. This is simply the appointment of a *National No-Accident Day*. Not a month or a week but *one day*. It could be a day announced, say, six to eight weeks in advance, on which it should be a point of honour with each member of the population that he or she should not be involved in an accident on that *one* day. There would be concentrated propaganda by the Press, TV, radio, schools, Churches, and the Motoring and Pedestrians' Associations, etc., leading up to that *one* day. Is it too much to suppose that, on that one day, most people would take just a little more care than on other days? It would be too much to expect motorists to have posted on their windscreens a notice 'I will not have an accident today', but it would be a nice idea, as such a motorist might feel a little foolish when his car was found embracing a lamp post.

The difference between this suggestion and local or even national safety weeks is obvious. In the first place a week is much too long. People could concentrate on being careful for a day, but not at present for a week.

Secondly, of course, local safety weeks do not appeal to those passing through the locality. But, if subjected to intensive propaganda for a short period (not for too long, that is why six to eight weeks is suggested— possibly four would be even better), is it not possible that just on that one day the average person (who, after all, does not want fifteen people to be killed every day) would take a little extra care? And, if he did, the

result would probably be a marked drop in the accident
rate on that day.

It is not suggested that, if the test were successful, the
annual accident rate would immediately drop, but
would not an important step have been taken in that
direction by proving to the public what could be
achieved? And, at the worst, if only seven lives and
hundreds of bodies were saved that day, it could hardly
be counted a failure. The cost in advertising would have
been well spent.

As far as one can see, this is the only positive step
which can be taken, and can be taken at once, to halt
the accident rate. Is it not worth a trial? If it failed
completely what harm would it have done? No one is
going to behave more recklessly or more carelessly just
because a National No-Accident Day was a failure.

What argument is there against the suggestion? Only
the fact that this idea was tried out two years running
in the U.S.A. and failed each time. Of course that is a
matter to be considered, but the U.S.A. is a completely
different country from this one. It is vastly larger
and divided into States, and there is a great deal of
independence among the States. They have not the
same national Press or broadcasting systems as we
have. It may well be far harder for the central government to reach each individual in the Country there
than it is here. In those circumstances it could well be
that an attempt to run a national campaign there
might fail. If it had failed in one of the Scandinavian
countries there might be more reason for doubt as to
its success. If this country hesitates to try it itself, why
could it not join with the Scandinavian countries, put

the names in a hat, and agree that one country should
try the experiment?

There is so little to lose and so much to gain that it is
difficult to understand why the suggestion has not been
put into practice. Schemes for better roads are talked
about and slowly put into operation, advice is given to
the motorist and to the pedestrian, letters are written
to the papers suggesting increased fines, disqualification
and imprisonment—but here is one positive suggestion
which might do good immediately. No other suggestion
which can be put into immediate effect has ever been
made.

No doubt it is considered in some quarters that the
public is too apathetic to respond, and that everyone
now accepts thousands of deaths and hundreds of
thousands of injuries on the roads as a normal incident
of modern existence. But ought such acceptance to be
acquiesced in? Is this not one chance of trying to break
it down? An attempt to break it down by this method
is at least better than leaving it to become a permanent
feature of modern life.

10 *Costs in Civil Cases*

COSTS in civil cases are always important and sometimes become the chief element in a case, particularly where the amount in dispute is small. And many complaints are heard about the cost of obtaining justice. There could today be some improvement in this respect but nothing like as much as is desirable.

The first unpalatable fact which the public has to realise is that lawyers have to be paid, and, if it wants good lawyers, it must pay them well. Without good lawyers the standard of the administration of justice would become deplorable. The judges must necessarily be drawn from lawyers, and unless persons are attracted to the legal profession by the hope of substantial material success, cases would be conducted badly by bad advocates before bad judges.

So, lawyers have to be paid well. In consequence litigation must be expensive. Is this an injustice or may it lead to injustice? Certainly. But the only remedy is for the public to bear the expense—or a large part of it. With the tremendous claims at present on the public purse, for defence, housing, health and the social services generally, and with the gradual realisation that there must be a limit to public expenditure, a suggestion that the State should bear the whole or a substantial part of the costs of private litigation would hardly be popular. Some of the expense is borne already, by reason of the Legal Aid and Advice Acts, but the amount involved is only a very small proportion of the amount spent on litigation generally.

Whenever the expense of litigation is being considered it is also important to keep the rights and wrongs of the matter in perspective. Charles Reade in one of his books makes a Yankee refer to English justice as 'Prime—but tarnation dear!' The employment of such highly-trained men as judges means a machine for righting serious injustice, not for securing to everyone the uttermost farthing of his rights. A sane rich man would not normally spend 20s. to recover 6d., and most wise people would avoid litigation if they can possibly do so. There is a danger, when the public is legally aided, that people may be assisted and encouraged to indulge in foolish litigation because they have in fact a legal right which a sensible man of means would not seek to enforce.

Apart from the complaint of the high cost generally, one of the main grievances of litigants is that, even if a case is won, the successful party seldom gets paid all his costs of winning the case. A simple example should show why it is impossible to remedy this entirely. Suppose in a fairly simple case a litigant instructs his solicitor to brief one of the leading Q.C.s in the country. The brief may be marked a thousand guineas. Counsel on the other side may be an able but less fashionable junior, whose fee is a hundred and fifty guineas. If the litigant who instructs the Q.C. wins, is he to be reimbursed by the losing party the full fee that he paid the fashionable Q.C., or only an amount sufficient to pay for a barrister of the same importance as his opponent? Most people would say the latter. But, in that case, a man who was shown to be in the right would have had to pay part of his own costs.

Although an extravagant example has been taken, the same sort of thing is going on all down the line. Suppose a man who is very proud of his driving record has an accident case in the County Court and the amount claimed is £100. The proud driver might employ a barrister who required thirty guineas to appear for him. If he won, he would be unlikely to recover more than about twelve from the other side. In the County Court there are fixed scales of costs and only in special circumstances can they be exceeded. Without extravagance it may be necessary to pay more than the amount fixed by the scales and normally in all such cases the winner has to pay something out of his own pocket.

This is what is meant by the difference between solicitor and client costs (i.e. what a client owes his own solicitor), and party and party costs (i.e. what one side has to pay the other by way of costs). The costs are fixed by a legal official and this is called taxation of costs. A client usually agrees his own solicitor's bill without taxation. The difference between party and party costs and solicitor and client costs always has to be paid by the client and cannot be recovered by him from the losing party in ordinary litigation.

Many people think that this is an injustice which should be remedied, at any rate to some extent, and it would certainly be possible to change the law so as to ensure that, provided a litigant did not indulge in extravagance, such as briefing a fashionable silk in a case which did not justify it, he should be paid all his costs by the other side. But, of course, care would have to be taken to see that this did not put an additional weapon into the hands of the rich man. He will always have the weapon of his wealth, in the sense that he may be able to afford to lose the case without noticing it, whereas his opponent will be greatly affected by losing it. But, if the rich man can also pile up the costs so that his poorer opponent has the prospect of paying a large bill if he loses, this would act as an unfair deterrent to the poorer man. It would, therefore, be necessary to frame any change of the present rule so as to prevent this sort of thing happening as far as possible. But unquestionably the fact that a losing party would have to pay higher costs would always be a factor in favour of his richer opponent.

None the less, in spite of these considerations, it would seem fairer that a man who wins his case should be paid (subject to reasonable safeguards as to extravagance) the whole of his costs by his unsuccessful opponent. This state of affairs could be achieved, and it is one of the reforms in the law which would remove an injustice and would not cost the public anything.

But that reform would still leave the inequities caused by the Legal Aid and Advice Act and these are far harder, if not impossible, to remove. At the moment, if a person's capital and income is sufficiently small to qualify him for a grant of legal aid, and if his case has sufficient apparent merits in law and in fact, he can proceed to trial with the knowledge that, as far as his own costs are concerned, he either has nothing to pay or a fixed amount (according to his financial position), and that, as far as his opponent's costs are concerned, he will not have to pay anything unless the judge specially orders him so to do. If the case is a reasonable one to fight, and if his conduct throughout has not been open to question, it is unusual for a judge to make him pay anything, even though he loses the case. And when he is ordered to pay a sum, it is practically always substantially less than the costs in fact incurred by his successful opponent.

It has been said that, although this is unjust to the successful litigant, he suffers no more than in a case where one side or the other has no means with which to pay his opponent's costs. In those cases, however, the State has not assisted either side.

It would therefore appear that the only remedy for this state of affairs is for the public to foot the bill, i.e. to provide a fund which should pay the costs of successful litigants if they cannot be recovered from a legally-aided person. It can fairly be said in such cases that, as the State has equipped the unsuccessful party to harass his opponent, either by maintaining a suit or defending it when he is in the wrong, the State should pay the costs of the successful party. This again is a reform which would remove an injustice and could be achieved, but this reform would cost the public money. Is it prepared and able to pay?

Not long ago a legally-aided plaintiff brought a case against several defendants which lasted for forty-one days. He lost it and, while his conduct was severely criticised by the judge, the defendants were completely exonerated. Nevertheless they had to pay their own costs themselves. That obviously is not justice, but it must be remembered that, if the State is to reimburse those defendants, it must reimburse all other successful parties whose opponents were legally aided, unless there are special circumstances. And the question, and really the only question, is—can the State afford it? If it can, in spite of the other calls on the public purse, it should pay, but, if it cannot, the injustice will have to remain. Even if a fund is established for the purpose of re-imbursing such parties, rules will have to be made to prevent unfair advantage being taken of it, but this should not be too difficult. However, when all this has been done, it will still leave out in the cold the person who wins an action against someone who is not legally aided and who cannot pay the costs.

11 *The Law's Delays*

BETWEEN the wars it was common experience for litigants and their legal representatives to spend a day or more in a County Court without their cases even being reached, let alone tried. It was by no means an isolated example for a claim for about £10 not to be tried until the parties had attended on four separate days, with an interval of several weeks between each attendance. And they had to wait the whole of each of the three days before the judge would allow them to go home. Moreover long cases might be heard with intervals of weeks or even months between the various hearings. In such circumstances it is difficult if not impossible for a judge to have a proper grasp of a case, even if he takes a particularly thorough note. He cannot be expected to remember the effect which each witness made on his mind even if the witness's actual words are written down.

Fortunately, however, that sort of thing in the County Court is becoming a thing of the past. The County Court is indeed becoming very near to an ideal court, as some courts already try cases with no delay at all and always on the days fixed for them. If a case requires more than one day it can usually be given two or more days in succession. The reason for this is that the Lord Chancellor, accepting the report of a Working Committee presided over by His Honour Judge Sir Alun

Pugh, arranged for the appointment of a number of additional judges. As each court has at least two court-rooms and some rooms which can exceptionally be used as courts, some County Courts now have enough judges and enough courts, and these two conditions will soon ensure a satisfactory judicial system. There are, of course, some courts, especially in the country, where difficulties still arise, but it is obvious that the problem of litigation in the County Courts has been solved in some courts and will, in time, be solved in all.

The situation in some County Courts is as follows. A case is fixed for hearing on a day normally from three to six weeks from the date when the summons is issued. If the parties want longer time they can, of course, have it. If it is urgently necessary that a case should be tried out of its turn this can always be arranged, even if several days are required for the trial of the case. Cases are always heard on the days fixed for them, and if a case is not finished on the first day it will continue on the next day, or upon the earliest day convenient to the parties. Long cases are never spread over weeks or months but are heard from day to day unless the parties wish otherwise.

In June 1960 the Law Society issued a report complaining of delays and adjournments in County Courts and suggesting the creation of a Central London County Court. The report certainly reads as though it had been made before the effect of the appointment of additional County Court judges had been appreciated. If there are still Courts in London where the days of the hearing of a long case are spread over weeks or months, that is a situation which, of course, needs remedying, as the Law Society's report says. A Central London County Court would certainly be one form of remedy for such an unsatisfactory state of affairs. But with the appointment of the additional judges it is quite unnecessary for cases to be spread over in the manner referred to. What one court in London can do the next can do also. If necessary a few extra judges could be appointed. The cost would be nothing compared with the erection and manning of a Central London County Court. Such a Court would also involve some litigants and witnesses in far too much travelling. The County Court is the Court where comparatively small cases are heard and it is desirable that they should be heard locally.

The happy state of affairs which either already exists or will exist in the County Court does not exist in the High Court. It is true that once a case starts there it will usually go on from day to day until it is finished. But there is a long delay before cases are heard and unless a day is fixed for a case (and this involves additional delay before the case is heard) the parties and their witnesses may wait in Court all day without the case being reached.

The reason for this delay and inconvenience is simply because the High Court has not enough judges *and* not enough courts.

Many attempts have been made to avoid delay and inconvenience in the High Court, but they were all doomed to failure and they all failed. The remedy is the same as in the County Court—more judges and more courts—but unfortunately it is not simple to apply the remedy. It may be that Parliament would sanction the creation of, say, five or six more High Court judges and, if there were courts available for them to sit in, the problems of delay and inconvenience would be automatically solved. But there are not the court-rooms in the Royal Courts of Justice. Even today small rooms which were never meant for courts are being used to supplement the proper Courts, and there are still nothing like enough.

It is accordingly a matter of money and priority in building. There is still an acute shortage of houses in London. There are still not enough beds for patients in the hospitals. Who is to have priority? That is a matter for Parliament and the public to decide. There is no doubt but that, if a sufficient building programme in and adjacent to the Law Courts were sanctioned, and if six new High Court judges were appointed the problem of delay and inconvenience in the High Court would be virtually solved. And, unless something of the kind is done, that problem never will be solved. Those responsible will no doubt make valiant attempts to find palliatives, but that is all they will be at the best, and it lies solely in the hands of Parliament and the public whether the provisions of Magna Carta are to be fulfilled as far as delay is concerned.

It is quite true that, if there were the extra judges and courts referred to, judges would from time to time be out of work, but the wasted judge-hours would be a small price to pay for the convenience both to the lawyers and the litigants. It is true that judges have been heard to complain at being left without any work owing to a sudden compromise of an action at the doors of the Court. But, although it is, of course, desirable

I

that cases should be settled as early as possible so as to avoid unnecessary expense and also so as to avoid places being taken unnecessarily in the list of cases to be tried, nevertheless in many cases it may not be possible to settle on terms satisfactory to both parties until the very last moment. And, after all, it is the parties' litigation, and it is their interests which matter most. The Courts and the judges are there for the convenience of the parties and not *vice versa*.

.   .   .   .   .

Since this chapter was written a Bill has been placed before Parliament to provide for an increase in the number of Court of Appeal and High Court judges (See Lord Justice Devlin's foreword at page 8). It will be interesting to see what provision will be made for extra Courts in which they can sit.

12 *References*

I Have knone Mrs Jones for 12 yers. She is
onest, hardworking, and truthful, and never
brakes anything. Noing her as I do I cannot
well say less.

(Signed) Mrs A. M. Brown.

IT IS not generally known that for a servant to forge a
reference in order to obtain employment is a very
minor offence indeed. It is punishable only with a small
fine, and there are very few such prosecutions today.
Forged references indeed present very few problems.
They are usually obvious, like the one quoted above or,
alternatively, they call for some enquiry which leads to
disclosure. There are, of course, some real criminals who
have access to typewriters, good notepaper and even
reasonable spelling, and who procure employment for
one of the gang by this means in order to rob a house or
a works safe, but a little investigation of a reference will
usually show whether it is genuine or not. And, if a man
chooses to act on a reference without assuring himself
of its genuineness, what follows is usually his own
fault.

The real problem, which both lawyers and the public
have to face, concerns the giving of references. It is often

not easy to decide for oneself what to do, nor is it always easy for a lawyer to advise satisfactorily. Indeed, scrupulous people may be involved in considerable difficulties over the matter of references, and they may even be involved in considerable legal expense without any fault on their side. Should a reference be given at all? And, if it is to be given, in what terms?

No honest person will give an unfair reference, that is to say a reference which is either unfair to the person about whom it is written or to the person who is going to be asked to rely on it. But the temptation to be dishonest is in certain circumstances considerable. It may save a lot of trouble and even a lot of money. Suppose, for example, a man has an employee whose honesty he greatly suspects but against whom he can prove nothing. Things are constantly disappearing and the employer knows that no one else can have taken them although theoretically that could have happened. He could, of course, call in the police and set a trap for the person concerned. It may be that it is his duty to do so. But most people shrink from discharging such a duty and it is difficult to attach much blame to them. So, instead of taking this unpleasant course, he gives proper notice to determine the employment.

Now what is going to happen about a reference? The employer can, of course, say: 'Don't ask me for a reference,' for no one is bound to give one. But, if the employee is in fact dishonest, the employer may well be asked why a reference is refused. The employer will incur no risk of legal proceedings by answering this question truthfully if no one else is present, but if in someone else's presence he says: 'Because we believe

you have been stealing regularly from us,' there is
nothing to prevent the employee from bringing an
action against him for slander in the High Court of
Justice. The employer will doubtless win the action and
the employee will be ordered to pay his costs of at least
£200, but, as the employee will be unable to comply
with the order, the employer will in fact have to foot
the bill himself. Much cheaper to pay the employee
£25 and be done with it.

But suppose the employer either parries the question
or, if he tells the truth, says it to the employee when no
one else is present? The employee then passionately
asserts innocence and defies him to make the same
statement when a reference is applied for. Now what is
the employer going to do? In due course a letter is
written to him asking for a reference and enclosing a
stamped addressed envelope for reply. Does he just
ignore it? This will seem extraordinarily rude to the
person who asks for it. Does he telephone instead? If
so, what does he say when asked: 'Is X honest?' Or, if
the employer opens the proceedings by saying he won't
give a reference, what explanation does he give for
refusing? Or does he hang up with apparent rudeness?
It is almost impossible to say anything honestly to the
enquirer which, if repeated to the employee, could not
be capable of meaning, or at least be twisted into
meaning, something against the character of the
employee. And, once the employer has done that, an
action may be brought against him for damages. He
will always win such an action if he has said nothing
unfair and provided his only object is to refrain from
giving an unfair reference. But it will be small comfort

to win when he has to pay his solicitor's bill of £200 or more and know that he will never get a penny of it back.

Let us assume that all this has happened, that the employer has spoken the truth from the start, that he has refused to let a new employer take on an employee whose honesty is gravely suspect, and that in consequence he is the loser by £200 or more. May he not say to himself: 'If only I'd given a false reference from the start none of this would have happened. I should have been saved worry and expense'?

Well, it may be he would say this, but it is far from certain. For, if he had taken that easy course, his conscience or whatever he calls it might have given him some nasty moments. Moreover, if he has any imagination he might have wondered how many teaspoons disappeared from the house where X went to work, thanks to the false reference. He might feel a little uncomfortable about that. But there could be much worse to come. If X's new employer discovered that X was dishonest the previous employer might be called upon to account for his reference. And then, if he told the truth, he would be liable to a real action being brought against him, an action for fraud. That is to say that, if he admitted that he did not believe his statement that X was honest to be true, X's new employer could claim from him any loss suffered as a result of taking on X in consequence of the false reference. And in this action he would not only have to pay his own costs of at least £200, but the new employer's costs as well (amounting to at least the same sum), and some damages too, possibly very heavy damages (if, for example, X has had bigger ideas and made away with something of real value). But perhaps he will avoid the costs by paying damages straight away.

After that action the first employer might sit down and say: 'What a pity I didn't give a truthful reference. That would only have cost me £200.' Or, of course, he might say: 'What a pity I didn't lie again when X's employer complained of the reference and say that I had every reason to believe X to be completely honest.' Yes, probably, if he had given a false reference and lied about it afterwards, he would have got away with it, though that sort of conduct doesn't appeal to most people. But, in case it does, he should realise that, even in that case, he is not absolutely safe, because the dishonest servant might even try to blackmail him by threatening to tell the new employer of the dishonest reference.

Yes, life can be difficult for people who give or refuse references. Fortunately the consequences described above very rarely happen, but they may. One really needs a lawyer to advise at every stage of the proceedings, but then again he will have to be paid, and on such a delicate, difficult matter he may give the wrong advice.

Some people may think that the moral of this chapter is this: 'Whatever I do or refrain from doing may land me in difficulty or expense. At least, therefore, I want the moral satisfaction of having told the truth to the best of my ability and that is the line I shall take for better or worse.'

But just suppose the servant really was honest and it

was all a horrible series of coincidences! Think of the harm you will have done to that unfortunate employee if you convey your mistaken but genuine belief to the prospective employer!

The only way in which the situation of references could be improved would be if it were provided by legislation that in any case of an action for libel or slander, where the occasion was *prima facie* privileged, no action should be allowed to proceed, unless the plaintiff satisfied the Court (or the defendant admitted) that there was some evidence of malice on the part of the defendant.

13 *On Being Reasonable*

You will not be able to spend any appreciable time in the Law Courts without hearing some reference to the reasonable man, woman, child and even domestic animal. But there is only one test of reasonableness in such animals. If they bite or kick, they are acting unreasonably—unless it is entirely in fun. No one, of course, objects to being lifted out of the stable by the hind legs of his favourite hunter or bitten to the bone by the Scottie which shares the bed—provided it isn't meant as an act of unkindness. If it happens to be someone other than the owner who is the victim of the animal's exuberance it is, of course, explained at once that he or she doesn't actually dislike strangers but has to get to know them first. So it is simple enough for a domestic animal to be reasonable. It has to obey one rule only—not to be vicious.

But the standard for man and woman and, to a lesser extent, child is a far more exacting one. Where a duty to be reasonable exists, the law will have regard to a person's age and sex but, subject to this qualification, at no time during the existence of the duty may he or she fall below the required standard. Their driving, for example, must always be careful—at no moment must they take their eyes off the road, drive too fast or back into their neighbour's pram. (And here let it be said emphatically that the reference to the law taking account of sex does not mean that there is one standard of driving for the lady and another for the gentleman. It may be that she finds parking the car rather more difficult than he does, it may be that reversing and turning round—perhaps even due to her inferiority in physical strength—cause her considerable anguish, but this will be no excuse when she scrapes the paint off the wing of a car within striking distance.) And in walking, too, the reasonable person always looks where he or she is going, never steps backward without first turning round, moves only as fast in the dark as is safe, and never trips over a stone which he or she should have seen.

If, as a result of a failure to take these elementary precautions, you fall into a well or a river or a lime-kiln, the law will say that justice has been done. But it is not only out of doors that this high standard of behaviour must be maintained. The reasonable man never spills his beer, nor the reasonable woman her tea or gin. They never play the wireless too loud, lose their temper (unreasonably), leave their umbrellas or suit-cases in omnibuses or taxis, or do anything which a reasonable man or woman would not do, or omit to do anything which a reasonable man or woman would do. It is useless for the octogenarian to contend that, up till the one moment which is the subject matter of a lawsuit in which he is involved, he has acted reasonably every second of his life. Eighty years' unblemished record will serve him not a jot. He must pay damages. He has omitted to do that which a reasonable octo-genarian would do or he has done that which a reasonable octogenarian would not do.

But what about the judge who holds the octogenarian liable? What are his duties and liabilities? Far heavier than those of the ordinary reasonable man. For not only has he in his private life to come up to the same standard of reasonableness as the accountant or coal-heaver who lives next door to him, but he has his duties in Court as well. There he has to expound and apply the law of the reasonable man to and for the benefit or alternatively to the complete humiliation of his fellow men. One might have thought that English law—judge-made as so much of it is—would have allowed a little licence to its unfortunate judges who are compelled to dole out reasonableness day after day, week after week. Toffee for breakfast, toffee for dinner and toffee for tea, complained the Duke in *Patience*—you can have too much even of toffee. Think of the poor judge, imprisoned on his Bench from 10.30 to 1 and from 2 to 4.15, five days a week for at least thirty-eight weeks in the year. Surely he can be allowed a little unreason in the hours he spends away from his prison?

Not at all. He must keep his place in the queue like everyone else; he must not leave litter in the street—not even the torn-up sketches he made during counsel's final speeches; when driving, he must leave pedestrians, who are on a pedestrian crossing, well alone. From his Bench in Court he may tell a witness to stand up and behave himself and take his hands out of his pockets, and any back-answer by the witness could be rewarded by arrest and imprisonment. Yet, should the judge let his very natural feelings get the better of him after an instance of bad driving—by someone else, of course—to such an extent that in the purple vernacular he tells

the offending driver what he very properly thinks of
him, he himself will be liable to be arrested for conduct
likely to cause a breach of the peace or for using
insulting words and behaviour in a public place. And if
this happened, the reasonable judge would be brought
up before a reasonable magistrate and subjected, no
doubt, to a reasonable fine. But this is just a happy
pipe-dream. It doesn't happen. The reasonable judge
is so used to acting reasonably in Court that he is
incapable of doing anything else outside it.

In Court he sits and listens—always awake—never
allowing his attention to wander, never being prejudiced by the unprepossessing appearance of the
plaintiff or the demure and rather charming ('Perhaps
you would like to sit down, madam') looks of the
defendant, never giving a hasty or rash judgment,
never, never losing his temper, never being affected in
his mind by a most prejudicial piece of inadmissible
evidence which somehow slipped out during the
proceedings, and, of course, always disclosing that he
has one share in the British Transport Commission's
undertaking, before trying a running down case in
which the Commission is involved.

But there is one mistake he is allowed to make. This
may surprise the public who assume that, if lawyers
don't know the law, at any rate judges should. Well, so
they should and quite often do, but they *are* allowed to
make mistakes in law.

Yes, the reasonable omnibus driver must make no
mistakes in driving, but the reasonable judge may make
mistakes in law. His mistakes may cost the parties a lot
of money, but, although his decision may be reversed

in the Court of Appeal and although its decision may be reversed in the House of Lords, the salary and position of all the judges concerned remain intact. For the truth is that, although all the law is locked up in the breasts of the judges, it is not expected to come out in all circumstances from all judges. The reasonable man never omits to do anything which a reasonable man would do. But one reasonable judge—in his judicial capacity—may omit to do something which another reasonable judge would do. And, indeed, who is to say which of two reasonable judges is the more reasonable? The reasonable judge of first instance says that, in his view, the plaintiff is in the right. Champagne is drunk by the plaintiff and his legal advisers. Three reasonable judges in a most reasonable Court of Appeal say that, in their view, the defendant was in the right. Champagne is drunk by the defendant and his legal advisers. Five reasonable judges in the most reasonable of all Houses of Lords say that, in their view, it has not been proved that anyone was in the right and the thing should start all over again. On this occasion only the legal advisers on each side can afford to drink champagne.

Many lawyers will tell you that litigation is a mug's game. Should reasonable men, then, go to law at all? If they didn't, there would be no reasonable judges. And, if there were no reasonable judges, there would be no reasonable men. Would the world be poorer? The inside of omnibuses would certainly be overcrowded, for the reasonable man has sometimes been referred to as a man on *top* of the Clapham omnibus. The idea that reasonable men never went inside is odd, particularly as when the phrase was first used the tops of omnibuses were uncovered. Possibly it had something to do with smoking, for not even a reasonable judge can smoke inside an omnibus without the certainty of ejectment. Disclosure of his office would make no difference.

'D'you know who he is? He's a judge of the High Court!'

'Well—he wouldn't allow smoking in his Court, and I don't in my bus.'

Poor, reasonable judge; but perhaps there are compensations, if only in his private dreams when he pictures himself doing all the unreasonable things he has never done and omitting to do all the reasonable things he has always done. And if these glorious thoughts in his subconscious mind make him snore and his wife, that reasonable little woman by his side, wakes him up to call attention to the offence, does he strangle her or strike her with the back of his hand? Not at all.

'If I were to strike you, my dear,' he says, 'it would be an assault, and might amount to cruelty. There was a case I had the other day——'

'Oh, do let me go to sleep, George,' says the reasonable little woman, very reasonably.

14 *Imprisonment for Debt*

IN 1869 Mr George Jessel, a Member of Parliament (later Sir George Jessel, Master of the Rolls), said: 'I trust that at some not long distant time public opinion will be in favour of the abolition of imprisonment for debt altogether.'

He was speaking during a debate in the House of Commons while the Debtors Act 1869 was being considered as a Bill.

This Act was described in its preamble as 'An Act for the abolition of imprisonment for debt', and was designed to put an end to the state of the law against which Dickens and others campaigned, under which a creditor who had obtained a judgment against a debtor could have the debtor imprisoned until the debt was paid—which, in many cases, was for ever. And since 1869 the scandal of the debtors' prison has disappeared.

That Act, however, still preserved a power in the Courts to send a judgment debtor to priosn for a limited period on certain conditions. It was against the retention or creation of this power that Mr Jessel was speaking. Almost everyone was then agreed that imprisonment for debt, as it had been practised up till then, should be abolished, but people were not agreed as to whether the Courts should retain *any power at all* to send judgment debtors to prison simply for not paying the debt.

The 1869 Act provided that a judge could send a judgment debtor to prison for a maximum period of six weeks provided, and provided only, it was established that the debtor could have paid the amount in respect of which he had made default, i.e. if the judgment was that he should pay the whole amount, the creditor would have to prove he could have paid this *whole* amount, but if the judgment was that the amount should be payable by periodical instalments the creditor need only prove that he could have paid one or more of the instalments.

It is remarkable what up-to-date arguments were used in both Houses of Parliament during the debates which led to the passing of this Act, although they took place nearly a hundred years ago, and it may be interesting to set out some of these arguments in the words of the people concerned. The main division of opinion was this. Mr Jessel and those who thought with him considered that a creditor under an ordinary contract should never have the power to put a debtor in prison merely for non-payment of a debt. If credit had been obtained fraudulently the criminal law could deal with the man. But if credit was obtained honestly and was given voluntarily, indeed, in some cases, pressed on the debtor, in no circumstances should the debtor be liable to go to prison even if it was some extravagance which prevented him from paying his creditor. It was pointed out that a man of some means could always avoid going to prison by the simple expedient of paying £10 and going bankrupt. There is no need to give credit at all, they argued, and if a creditor chooses to give credit where it is not due, so much the worse for him. Preserving this power of imprisonment, they said, is to preserve something which in many cases will cause one law for the rich and another for the poor.

On the other hand, those in favour of the present terms of the Act argued that, unless there were some sanction of imprisonment, debts could not be collected and credit would never be obtainable by the poorer people, so that those provisions of the Act were really to their advantage.

Here are some extracts from the speeches during the progress of the Bill:

The Attorney-General (Sir R. P. Collier) *said that it was a process of imprisonment for the purpose of compelling the payment of a debt. He had had a conference with the County Court judges and he found that they were almost unanimous in favour of maintaining the power of imprisonment as they thought that the Courts could not be worked without them. . . . Many men would not pay their debts until the order of committal was made out . . . and he had received deputations not only from the County Court judges and trading associations but also on behalf of the working classes themselves, stating that if once abolished their credit would be gone and credit to a poor man was almost a necessity of his existence. For these reasons he had come to the conclusion that this power of imprisonment should be maintained.*

(Note: The County Court judges today would certainly not be 'almost unanimous' on the matter.)

Mr McLean: *The great argument against abolition of imprisonment was that it would put a stop to credit and materially interfere with trade but as a manufacturer he*

K

*wished it would. Any honest man could get credit in a legiti-
mate manner at any time and it would be a great advantage to
the working man if the means of obtaining credit would be
limited. The working men were inveigled into debt in order
that the shopkeepers might have a hold on them for the continu-
ance of their custom. To curtail credit by abolishing imprisonment for debt would be a great advantage to the working classes.*

Mr McMahon *said that when arrest on mesne process*[1]
*was abolished . . . it was then said that credit would be
disturbed and that traders would not be able to carry on their
business. But these forebodings were purely imaginary. If,
however, they allow the rich man to escape under the bankruptcy system they ought not to permit the poor man to be liable
to imprisonment . . . at present the County Courts were converted into agencies for the collection of small debts, many of
which were incurred by the wives of poor men in consequence of
the importunities of traders . . . all political economists from
Adam Smith to Mill laid it down that it was not for the
interests of the State to encourage credit and he believed that, if
they were to abolish imprisonment for debt, trade would be all
the more flourishing and there would be less temptation to
embark on those speculations where the gains were their own
and their losses their creditors'. . . . Unless a fraud or crime is
committed it is not the province of society to interfere. . . . He
desired to withdraw the amendment*[2] *in deference to the opinion
of the Attorney-General, who, he believed, was working
diligently to secure the end he had in view and who in due time
would doubtless take the initiative in the matter.*

Sir Henry Hoare *said that the Bill should be called not a*

[1] This was a procedure by which a debtor could be arrested even
before judgment was given against him.

[2] This was an amendment, the object of which was to abolish imprisonment for debt altogether.

bill for the abolition of imprisonment for debt but a bill for the extension of imprisonment for debt.

(Note: A slight excess of enthusiasm here perhaps but it shows how little Parliament has changed.)

Mr Anderson *said that the plea that imprisonment was for contempt of court was a transparent fiction because it was impossible for the County Court judges with the immense amount of work devolving on them to enquire so minutely into cases as was necessary for a just decision.*

County Court judges today certainly have time (and use it) to enquire into each case and no man is sent to prison just because the judge has no time to look into his case thoroughly. On the other hand, the imprisonment is only ordered *at the request of the creditor.* If the creditor takes no action, neither can the judge. How different if tomatoes were thrown at a judge by a debtor! The creditor (who had perhaps suffered under that particular judge for years) might be delighted and ask the judge to disregard the matter.

CREDITOR: I'm sure he didn't mean it, your Honour.

JUDGE: Then why did he bring a tomato with him into the witness box?

CREDITOR: It may have given him confidence, your Honour.

JUDGE: Really, Mr Slope, I shall commit you to prison as well if you're not careful.

In such a case the judge has, of course, the power to commit to prison, whether the creditor wants it or not. That is real contempt of court. The object of the power of imprisonment in the Debtors Act is to enable the judge in proper cases to pass a sentence of imprisonment for the benefit of the creditor. This sentence the judge is given power to suspend and it is always suspended so long as the debtor pays within a certain period or pays so much a week or so much a month. That is what the creditor wants. He wants the debtor to pay for fear of imprisonment and in order to avoid it. If, however, a judge ordered a debtor to pay a debt within a certain time and it was plain from the debtor's evidence that he could pay it easily, and if later it transpired that he had not paid it, the judge could do nothing about it unless the creditor took the necessary proceedings against the debtor.

Mr Morley *said that he should be glad to put an end to imprisonment for debt at once and for ever. It belonged to the dark ages. . . . He believed, however, that the people were not quite prepared for the entire abolition of imprisonment for debt.*

(Note: Are they so prepared ninety years later?)

Mr West *said that in consideration of the fact that general opinion was progressing in favour of total abolition of imprisonment for small debts he thought it would be inexpedient to press the amendment[1] to a division.*

Lord Romilly *deprecated the power of imprisonment for debt in the hands of County Courts. He believed the power of imprisonment for debt was very injurious. Credit was given for goods sold in the ordinary way only because the vendor believed the purchaser would be able to pay and not because he thought he should be obliged to have to resort to compulsory measures; and the fear of imprisonment benefited no one but the tallyman who was thereby enabled to force his goods on the unwary poor and relied almost exclusively on the compulsory power of imprisonment.*

[1] See second footnote to page 146.

(Note: To the tallyman can be added credit sales and hire-purchase transactions arranged by canvassers or induced by attractive advertisements.)

Mr Anderson *said that the fear that the working classes would be unable to get credit if power of imprisonment was abolished was groundless, because they would continue to get credit on the only proper basis, that of good character, and the abolition would have the good effect of putting a stop to the tally system.*

Mr West *said that he believed it to be the right view and was fortified in that view by the opinion of Lord Abinger who said 'a man of good character could always get credit; if his character was bad he did not deserve to have any and it was better he should not be trusted at all . . .' He admitted that probably the country was not ripe for the abolition of imprisonment for debt altogether, and he would support the Attorney-General's Bill reserving to himself the right to move the total abolition of imprisonment for debt when he should find the country in favour of it.*

(Note: Mr West obviously died first.)

Mr Henley *said that the Attorney-General had justified his proposal by the opinions of County Court judges but those who had lived some time in the world would remember when a man might be hanged for stealing a shilling's worth and plenty of learned judges gave it as their opinion that it would be impossible to say what might happen if this penalty were taken away. . . . As to stopping credit he did not believe that the abolition of imprisonment would have any such effect.*

The Attorney-General *also said that he had been informed by the County Court judges in references to orders for imprisonment that not one in fifty really took effect and that with respect to the class of persons appearing in the County*

Court the provision of the power of imprisonment was abso-
lutely necessary to ensure the payment of debts.

(Note: Latest figures today show that something like
1 in 17 or 18 goes to prison under these orders. In 1957
63,570 committal orders were made and 2,539 debtors
went to prison. In 1958 the figures were 76,714 and
4,160 and in 1959 93,018 and 5,355.)

Lord Romilly *later said that he admitted that all or*
nearly all the judges of the County Courts are strongly in
favour of preserving to them that power, but they were not in his
opinion the best judges.

Mr Roden *said that as an extensive employer of labour he*
considered that the honest man would always be able to get
credit and that the facility of obtaining credit was frequently
a disadvantage rather than a gain to the poor.

(Note: Although there were no radios, television sets
or motor cars in those days.)

Mr Jessel *said later that although he should vote for the*
proposal . . . yet he confessed that for a long time his own
opinion had been in favour of abolishing imprisonment for
debt and as a question of general policy he believed that the
majority of people were prepared to support total abolition. He
believed that it was a mistake for people to imagine that with
the removal of the power of committal for debt the practice of
giving credit would also cease. The same thing was said when
arrest on mesne process was abolished and he believed the
objection now urged to be as much without foundation as it was
then. Perhaps until it was possible to get the public mind to
advance as far as to say that in no case should a man suffer
penal imprisonment because he failed to pay a sum of money
under a private contract with which the public had nothing to do,
the proposal of the Attorney-General was the best that could be

adopted. He trusted, however, that in some not very distant period public opinion would be in favour of the abolition of imprisonment for debt altogether.

The Attorney-General *said he should be glad if he could do so to abolish even this power of imprisonment but public opinion was not ripe for such a measure.*

(Note: It does not appear to have ripened in over ninety years.)

Today all the County Courts in England deal regularly with judgment summonses. The figures given above show that the percentage of debtors actually going to prison is increasing. In 1957 it was 1 in 25, in 1958 1 in 18/19 and in 1959 1 in 17/18. In spite of the anxiety of many Members of Parliament in 1869 that this power of imprisonment should be abolished as soon as possible, there is no agitation for its removal. Nevertheless the question does arise as to whether it is desirable that it should be retained.

In cases where credit has not voluntarily been given, in claims for rent and in the case of torts or the costs of legal proceedings it may well be that some ultimate power of imprisonment must always remain. Otherwise, for example, a man who was ordered to pay £20 damages for assault could not be made to pay even though he was capable of doing so. He might be earning a substantial weekly wage but have no property on which execution can be levied, and, apart from the creditor's right under the 1869 Act, he could laugh at the judgment. That obviously is a highly undesirable state of affairs. But it is quite a different matter when one man has voluntarily given credit to another. It is quite true that the man can only be sent to prison on proof that he could have paid, but that means that if a man, who has incurred the debt, is a little extravagant after judgment has been given against him, he is liable to be sent to prison. A man who incurs debts on a larger scale and consoles himself with a visit to the races when his creditors start to pursue him, can quite cheerfully file his petition in bankruptcy if the horses don't win often enough. It would probably be fair to say that almost all of the 5,355 debtors who went to prison in 1959 were people who were not very highly-paid weekly wage-earners.

It may be that the State and local authorities must collect taxes and rates by means of imprisonment if necessary. But is it desirable that a mere breach of contract should have the same result, even though it is accompanied by some extravagance? To decide whether a man has the 'means to pay' the Court has to consider a man's weekly income and expenditure. What is his rent? How many children has he got? And so forth. Of course he shouldn't rent a television set while he owes money to someone else. But should he be liable to go to prison if he does? And it must be remembered that, in order to avoid going to prison, he must pay certain instalments. This involves cutting down his expenditure. It is fairly certain that in many cases, if a man smokes, he is not going to cut down that item. So he has to take it out of the housekeeping and his wife and children get less food. And all this is because someone tempted the wife to buy on credit a vacuum cleaner which she couldn't really afford.

There is a completely different aspect of the matter. In the normal way the only people who really benefit from the issue of a judgment summons (which is the name of the proceedings for committing a debtor to prison) are the traders who do a lot of work of this kind, credit drapers and so on. The creditor with a single debtor or only one or two seldom gains by instructing his solicitor to issue a judgment summons. Here is a fictitious account of such a matter.

At the offices of a firm of solicitors a client is being interviewed:

SOLICITOR: Well, Mr Baines, I'm glad to tell you that we've got judgment in both your cases.

BAINES: With costs?

SOLICITOR: Oh, certainly.

BAINES: That's fine. What does it come to?

SOLICITOR: Let me see. In Smith's case it's altogether £26 5s. 6d., and in Brown's £27 18s.

BAINES: Thank you very much indeed. You have been quick. I always thought the law was so slow. I shall be able to tell people a different story when I hear that old tale in future. It's just prejudice, that's what it is. Well, I wonder if you could let me have a cheque for the money? It would come in quite handy. Let me see—it's £54 3s. 6d., isn't it? And I let you have £10 on account. As they've paid my costs I can have that back, I suppose?

SOLICITOR: I'm afraid there's a slight misunderstanding. I haven't got the money yet—except your £10—which I shall, of course, account to you for, though I'm afraid it may be eaten up by solicitor and client costs. I explained to you, I think, about that when you came.

BAINES: I expect so. I don't suppose I was really

listening. But what about this money—I thought you said you'd got it?

SOLICITOR: I said I'd got judgment for it. It isn't always quite the same thing, I'm afraid. But I'll start chasing them for the money. You'll be hearing from me.

During the next few months telephone calls take place between the client's and the solicitor's offices at intervals. For example:

CLIENT: This is Mr Baines speaking. May I speak to Mr Stone?

CLERK: I'm afraid he's out.

As a slight variation Mr Baines sometimes gets this:

CLERK: I'm afraid the gentleman attending to your matter is on holiday.

Or this:

CLERK: I'm afraid the gentleman attending to your matter is in conference with counsel. I'll ring you when he gets back.

And finally this:

SOLICITOR: I'm afraid I haven't very good news for you. Perhaps you'd better come to see me. No, not this afternoon. I'm full up. Tomorrow at 11? Very well.

So tomorrow at 11:

SOLICITOR: So sorry to have kept you waiting, Mr Baines. Just had a very difficult client.

CLIENT: I shall become one soon if you don't get me my money.

SOLICITOR: We can't do impossibilities, you know.

CLIENT: I'm owed over £50 and I want it. If I owed it, I'd have to pay it. I expect other people to do what I have to do.

SOLICITOR: I quite agree with you, Mr Baines, but

you can't get money out of a man if he hasn't got any.

CLIENT: How d'you know they haven't got any?

SOLICITOR: Well, we've tried every remedy so far, except a judgment summons. We put in execution. Everything on hire purchase or claimed by the wives. Nothing in their banking accounts except an overdraft. One of them says he's earning £500 a year, the other £650. One of them has a wife and two children, and the other a wife and three. Oh, yes, and the one with £650 has two elderly parents dependent on him.

CLIENT: What's this judgment summons you talk about?

SOLICITOR: Well, frankly, a judgment summons isn't much use unless either you know the debtor has got substantial means or unless you're one of the big stores and have a lot of them and get one solicitor to do them all for you. You see, the only costs a creditor can get, if he can get any at all (he often can't), are so small they simply don't pay in the ordinary way. They're usually more trouble than they're worth. In your case it isn't even as if both cases were in the same Court. One's at Croydon and the other at Ipswich. I'd have to get another solicitor or even counsel to do them for you and, in the end, you might well find it would cost you more than you'd get. Of course, if you could get a committal order you would eventually get your money but I very much doubt if you'd get one in either case.

CLIENT: Well, what do I do? Just laugh, or what?

SOLICITOR: The only alternative I can think of is to try to sell the debt to a debt-collecting agency.

CLIENT: What would they pay?

SOLICITOR: Can't be sure, but not much; 25 per cent perhaps—not more.

CLIENT: Just about pay the costs I've had.

SOLICITOR: With luck.

CLIENT: I'm fed to the teeth with the whole thing. It's three months now since I came to you and what have I got for it? Nothing—absolutely nothing . . . oh, yes, I have—I'll have your bill, I suppose.

SOLICITOR: I'll have it made out for you.

That sad little tale is no exaggeration and what happened was no fault of the solicitor. The client suffered two misfortunes, but they were both due to the debtors having insufficient means. If they had had sufficient means the client would have been able to get his money but he would still have had to bear the bulk of the costs of getting it, out of his own pocket. And that certainly would have been an injustice which could be remedied, if judgment creditors were given *all* their reasonable costs of trying to get their money.

But, while the judgment summons doesn't pay many creditors, it does pay the tallyman and the firms who have a lot of small debts, and, once they obtain a committal order against debtors, they are pretty certain of their money. But any debtor who is in danger of arrest for non-payment can always avoid imprisonment by paying £10 and filing his own petition in bankruptcy.

It may be wondered why the 5,355 people who went to prison in 1959 did not do that. The probable reason is that some of them were unaware of that solution, while many of them couldn't raise the £10. A few probably preferred to go to prison than go bankrupt because they were buying their house or owned property which they did not want to lose. But 87,663 people paid their debts rather than go to prison. If Sir George Jessel or some of his supporters in the Debate in 1869 heard of these figures they would presumably be disappointed. The present situation would seem to be that a number of the lower paid wage-earners go to prison because they have been guilty of some extravagance, while a good deal of money is spent uselessly on legal costs.

But the real question appears to be much the same as in 1869. If imprisonment for debt were absolutely abolished in cases where credit was voluntarily given would it unfairly or unsatisfactorily affect the giving of credit? The important words are unfairly and unsatisfactorily. Obviously credit would be more restricted and would in most cases be given only to those who deserved it. But would people who really needed it and to whom it ought to be given be deprived of it? With the much higher real wages that are paid today compared with those paid in 1869, and with the various benefits which are now distributed to people in need and which did not exist in 1869, it might well be that the consequent restriction of credit would help to check inflation and would be an advantage to the public as a whole. It is certainly doubtful whether the same bodies would make representations to the Government for its retention.

One of the questions which often arises before a judgment summons is issued is: to whom does the furniture and other personal property in a house belong? Before issuing a judgment summons, the

creditor usually tries levying execution on the debtor's
goods. Frequently on those occasions the wife or some
other relative of the debtor claims the goods and the
Court holds an enquiry to see to whom the goods do
belong. If the wife bought them, how did she get the
money with which to buy them? Was it part of the
housekeeping money? And so forth.

Where, however, the debt in respect of which execution is levied is for goods which are for the general
benefit of the household, it would perhaps not be
unreasonable if the goods of all members of the household were liable to execution in respect of the debt.
This would prevent subterfuges and it would seem to
be fair. As it is, if the husband owes money on a
television set and the creditor puts in execution, the
radio, gramophone or washing machine is claimed by
the wife or son or daughter. It would not be impossible
to provide that, where the debt was incurred for the
general benefit of the family, not simply for the personal benefit of the debtor, the family's goods as a whole
should answer for it. This would put a stop to the
frequent statement made by a bailiff—'Wife claims
all.'

Sometimes the goods claimed by the wife in fact
belong to the debtor, sometimes they belong jointly to
the debtor and his wife, sometimes they do genuinely
belong to the wife. But it is often very difficult for the
creditor to resist such claims successfully, and more are
allowed than disallowed. Few of them have much merit
because the debt is in respect of goods used by the
family as a whole and, if the claimant succeeds, it
means that the family keeps everything and, it may be,

without paying anything. If imprisonment for debt were abolished altogether it would certainly seem reasonable to amend the law relating to these claims and to provide that normally all the goods of the family should answer for any debt which was incurred for the family's benefit.

A further possibility would be to abolish imprisonment for debt where credit has voluntarily been given and to allow the attachment of earnings. This has recently been started in proceedings between husband and wife and, if that appears to work satisfactorily, it might be extended to other cases. It is a normal method of obtaining payment in Guernsey where there may be 'arrest of wages' up to one-half, though normally only a small proportion is awarded. It certainly seems more in keeping with modern thought that, where a man has committed no crime but owes money, money his or his goods rather than his body should be liable to seizure.

Perhaps one of the main objections to the attachment of earnings would come from the employers who would be involved in some expense, as they are with P.A.Y.E. It would appear quite unfair that the employers should be involved in any such expense. If that is to be avoided it would mean that, in order to attach earnings, the creditor would have to pay a fee for the benefit of the employer with the right ultimately to recover the fee from the debtor. It would still, however, mean that labour had to be utilised by the employer for wholly unproductive purposes as far as he was concerned.

On the 22nd August 1960 Mr Justice Danckwerts

wrote in a letter to *The Times*: 'There is a real case in my opinion for the abolition of imprisonment for non-payment of a debt.'

This letter was immediately followed by others, including one which emphasised that all the creditor wanted to do was to compel the debtor to pay by the fear of prison. It may be that the present procedure ought for other reasons to be continued, but the last argument hardly seems a good reason by itself for continuing it. The thumb-screw might prove an even more effective extractor, but no one would suggest that it should be used. The question is whether the threat of the loss of liberty in order to force payment of a civil debt where credit has voluntarily been given should be continued or whether it belongs, as was said in 1869, to the dark ages.

15 *Legal Integrity*

THERE is no doubt but that the standard of legal integrity in this country is very high. It is safe to say that judges are never bribed and that they never try cases where either of the parties is known to them, except possibly where both parties wish a judge to try a case and his acquaintanceship with one or other of them is purely superficial, or where no question of good faith or truthfulness could arise. Occasionally judges receive letters from foolish members of the public seeking to influence them, but no lawyer and no responsible member of the public would in any circumstances seek to do this. The worst that is ever said (or thought) of a judge is that he was unfair in a particular case. But even then it is not suggested that his unfairness was due to any improper motive. Even those few judges who in the past have been notorious for becoming biassed during the progress of a case were actuated by the best motives. They wanted to arrive at a correct decision and they wanted justice to be seen to be done. They just did not know how to set about it or were constitutionally incapable of doing so.

The judiciary could not possibly have achieved this reputation if it were not a fact that the legal profession as a whole has the highest standard of integrity. It is true that occasionally solicitors are guilty of financial dishonesty and barristers of gross misconduct. But the instances which are known are rare, and, though some misconduct must go unnoticed and, therefore, unpunished, there cannot be much of it.

But from time to time problems occur which give rise to difficulties, and occasionally the weaker members of both professions yield to temptation. There is often temptation because the impropriety which they resist, or to which they yield, is easy to commit and often appears to do no one any harm and the particular client a great deal of good.

For example, not very long ago a petitioner in a divorce case frankly admitted that she wanted a divorce from her husband and that, when he said he was going off to an hotel with a woman to commit adultery, and that he would send her the bill so that she could get a divorce, she readily agreed to his doing so. It would have been the simplest thing in the world for the petitioner's solicitor or counsel to persuade her to 'forget' that she ever said to her husband that she agreed to his suggestion. She need only have mentioned his statement in her evidence and either have added that she did not remember what she said in reply or that she said something like: 'Well, I suppose I can't stop you.' The petition was undefended, both parties wanted a divorce, and there must be solicitors and counsel who would have said to themselves: 'What harm can it do?' and have arranged for that dangerous piece of evidence either not to be given at all or to be so watered down that it became innocuous. In the particular case no such attempt was made. On the contrary the evidence was given freely and frankly and the petitioner would in consequence have failed to get a divorce, but for the fact that the petitioner's advisers were able to prove adultery by the husband prior to the conversation mentioned.

It is, however, very important indeed that such temptations should be sternly resisted. It is perfectly true that in any particular case no individual may suffer (indeed, in the case mentioned two individuals nearly suffered as a result of the integrity shown by the petitioner and her legal advisers) but the harm done to the profession as a whole would be very great, if the standard began to fall.

Here is a purely fictional case. A man is charged with capital murder and a great deal depends upon the cross-examination of one particular witness. According to the prisoner this witness is lying. Let it be assumed that the witness has claimed to have been at a particular theatre at a time when the prisoner says he was with the witness.

'You remember, then,' asks counsel, 'the comedian slipping on the stage and falling into the orchestra pit?'

'Very well,' says the witness incautiously.

Now, in fact, no comedian slipped on the occasion in question and the question was a grossly improper trap question. Presumably the witness was stupid or the trap would not have worked. But now what happens? It is conclusively proved that the comedian did not slip and the witness is shown to be the liar the prisoner claimed him to be. But for that one trap question the prisoner might have been convicted and hanged. What would happen to the barrister concerned?

One Bencher who was asked this question said: 'Nothing at all,' but that answer ought to be wrong. Once this type of misconduct were tolerated the standard of integrity would deteriorate appallingly. If counsel may tell deliberate lies[1] in the course of the case, that is an end of the trust which can be put in his word. And, once that trust disappears, the standard of integrity in the legal profession as a whole would drop to that of the countries where corruption is normal.

The argument for taking no action in that particular case is that the end justified the means, and that it is more important that an innocent life should be saved than that the integrity of a profession should be undermined. Undoubtedly the sanctity of human life is so great that it requires thought to deal with that argument. But, once it were conceded that, in a capital murder case, no holds were barred, why should not the same principle apply in a case where life imprisonment was the penalty? Such a punishment is considered worse than death by some people. And even a comparatively short term of imprisonment or a mere conviction might in some cases lead to the complete ruin of the accused person. A few weeks in prison might drive a claustrophobic insane. A few years in prison might result in a man's wife going on the streets and his children being put in a home. In other words, the result of a conviction of almost any kind may be almost as serious as a conviction for capital murder and may affect many more people, including innocent wives,

[1] The question asked by counsel was equivalent to his saying: 'During that performance the comedian slipped and fell. Do you remember the incident?'

parents and children. If, therefore, there is to be a complete freedom to counsel in the one case, why not in the others?

It is true that more latitude will be shown to counsel in a capital murder case because the consequences of conviction may be irremediable if a mistake has been made. But latitude is one thing, complete licence is another. It is reasonable latitude for counsel to be permitted to remind the jury of the consequences of conviction, but that is a very different thing from giving him licence to use any methods to get his client off.

It is accordingly suggested that, in the fictional case referred to, the Benchers of the Inn of the barrister concerned would be likely to censure him severely and to warn their members generally that such conduct cannot be tolerated, even for a good cause, and that any future offenders need not expect such leniency.

But, except in the case of undefended divorces (which constitute a unique form of litigation and which do involve legal advisers in temptation to break the rules), such temptations are comparatively rare.

A much more difficult problem arises when a barrister or solicitor is guilty of negligence. By negligence is meant not a wrong decision or wrong advice or wrong conduct of the case (all of which can occur without negligence) but a careless mistake causing loss or expense to the client. A simple example in the case of a solicitor would be the failure to give a notice in time; and in the case of a barrister the failure to look up a point in the appropriate law book and consequent wrong advice in ignorance of a definite decision of the Court to the contrary. These are simply examples but there is an infinite variety of ways in which a legal adviser can be careless and cause his client loss or expense.

Now the first question which arises is, does he always tell his client of his carelessness? And, secondly, does he make good the loss? In the case of a solicitor he is legally bound to make good the loss and can be sued if he does not do so. So presumably, where the solicitor confesses his fault fully to his client, he indemnifies him against his loss too. But are there cases where he conceals his fault? If there are, they are seldom, if ever, brought to light.

A barrister is, however, in a different position. He cannot sue for his fees and he cannot be sued for negligence. This has been the law for so long that it is unlikely to be changed, though it is difficult to justify it in principle. A Fellow of the Royal College of Physicians cannot sue for his fees but he can be sued for negligence, and the fact that medical men as a whole can be sued for negligence in no way seems to embarrass them in the discharge of their duties. Does the average surgeon stand with uplifted knife, wondering what the consequences of a mistake are likely to be? Yet more doctors are sued today than at any other time in their existence. This is in no way due to their being more careless but simply to the fact that it is today more easy to sue. In spite of these legal actions the standard of medicine and surgery appears never to have been so high.

Occasionally, it is believed, barristers have drawn cheques in favour of their clients to make up for some piece of carelessness, but it must be very rare. Undoubt-

edly the standard of care exercised by the Bar is very
high but there must always be some carelessness in
human affairs, and when it occurs on the part of a
barrister the question is, who is to pay for it? At the
moment it is the client who pays, except in the very
rare cases just mentioned.

Now there is one very serious argument against
barristers being made liable for negligence. Unquestionably if the law were changed so that they became
liable they would, like solicitors, insure against the
risk. Now, in the case of surveyors, many insurance
companies insist that, when a surveyor makes a report
on a house, he shall put in a clause approved by the
insurance companies with the object of limiting his
liability in the case of dry rot and similar defects. If
something similar were to happen in the case of
barristers it would be quite intolerable.[1] For example,
suppose at the end of every opinion the barrister had
to write:

'For the purpose of this opinion I have considered
all the cases which I can find but if by accident I have
omitted to look at any particular case and this opinion
is accordingly quite wrong I am not to be in any way
responsible for the consequences.'

It is essential that in giving an opinion or considering a case a barrister should not be fettered in any way
and it is equally essential that he should give his
definite and if possible unqualified opinion upon the
matter about which he is consulted. No doubt if

---

[1] The clauses put in by surveyors seldom, if ever, have the effect of
excluding legal liability for negligence, but their mere insertion would
make counsel's opinion of small value.

barristers became liable for negligence they would at first be able to obtain policies of insurance which did not contain any such obnoxious conditions. But suppose something equivalent to dry rot developed in the legal profession? In other words, suppose insurance companies found by experience that they were getting too many claims against their clients for one or two specific reasons (as they have found in the case of surveyors), might they not insist upon some clause like the dry-rot clause? For example: 'This opinion is only valid if the case is not heard before Mr Justice X.'

It is, of course, improbable that there would be many actions for negligence against barristers. The standard of care is very high. But this question of conditions in an insurance policy would have to be considered before any law imposing liability on barristers were passed. It is a formidable argument against any change. And it can further be argued that there is certainly no public clamour for a change, and that as, from the public point of view, the system seems to have worked well enough, it is as well to let it alone. Certainly there has been no agitation by solicitors to bring barristers into line with them in this respect, and it must in most cases be the solicitor who first becomes aware of any carelessness by the barrister whom he has briefed.

Whether or not the law is ever changed in this respect it is important that, if ever a barrister or a solicitor makes a careless mistake, he should inform the client of the fact. Motor accident insurance policies contain a clause which prohibit the insured from making any admission of liability. It would be intolerable if solicitor or barrister indemnity policies did the same thing.

There is a warning to new practitioners at the Bar which ought to have appeared in *Brief to Counsel*. It is that a barrister should never accept a brief in a highly specialised Court, e.g. in a patent action, unless (1) he is at least acquainted with the law and practice and procedure relating to the subject or (2) a specialist is briefed with him or (3) he discloses his complete ignorance both to the solicitor and to the client and advises them to brief someone else. If in spite of his taking the last-mentioned course he is pressed to take the brief he will have to do an infinite amount of work on the case and will probably make a mess of it, but at least this will be as much due to the stupidity of his client in persuading him to take the brief. Of course, if the lay client is of low mentality, thinks that all lawyers are much the same and does not really know what is happening, then the barrister should refuse the brief altogether.

It is not always appreciated by the public that a barrister is bound by legal etiquette to accept any case which he is free to take in any Court where he usually practises. He cannot properly refuse a case just because he thinks he is likely to lose it, though he will, of course, in such a case strongly advise the client either to settle it or abandon it. He is not, however, bound to take a case in a Court where he does not ordinarily appear, e.g. a copyright specialist need not accept an accident case and *vice versa*. And terrible things may happen if he is persuaded to accept the brief in such circumstances.

16 *Witnesses*

SOME people think and some judges have actually said that the present form of oath should be abolished and something simpler substituted, just 'I swear to tell the truth', for example. It is unlikely that unanimity among lawyers will be reached on this question. Undoubtedly some witnesses treat the oath as a mere formality and are as likely to tell the truth or not after taking it as they were before. But it certainly appears that some people are affected by the solemnity of the occasion and, as an incident at the end of this chapter records, its administration does have an effect sometimes.

But this is not a matter of great importance, although it would be a convenience to ushers in County Courts and Magistrates' Courts if a shorter form were used. At the moment they spend quite an appreciable time over the years correcting witnesses who insist on saying 'I swear by *the* Almighty God' or 'I swear by *my* Almighty God' instead of simply 'I swear by Almighty God'. Where the 'the' and 'my' come from no one seems to know, but it is as automatic with some people as the expression 'he *turned round* and said . . .'. He never just said. He always turned round first. So in fact did 'I' when 'I' replied to him.

More important than the actual words of the oath is

the general treatment of witnesses. Not everyone in Court appreciates the high state of nervousness in which an individual may be or that he is in fact an individual.

One of the characteristics of the first-class advocate is his ability to handle witnesses, either his own or his opponent's. The lesser advocates are inclined to treat witnesses like a fishmonger treats herrings. It's true that the fishmonger does say 'A *nice* pair of herrings for the lady', but no one would expect him to call for a nasty pair; and though, no doubt, there are sometimes differences, one dead herring is very like another. It may be that, when alive, they have, like human beings, their own personal idiosyncrasies, and perhaps one day someone will write a book *Living with Herrings* to match the experiences of Miss Len Howard, so charmingly described in her books *Birds as Individuals* and *Living with Birds*.

But that really is the point. Witnesses are alive, and are separate individuals, although there are certainly recognisable types of witness, such as the witness who enjoys giving evidence, the witness who is constitutionally incapable of telling the truth (unless he thinks it suits his purpose), and the witness who will say 'yes' to almost any question because he is so obliging.

The other day a deaf witness went into the witness box. The judge, in order to see how deaf he was, said very loudly: 'Can you hear what I say?' The witness turned towards the usher and said: 'What does he say? What does he say?' 'The judge wants to know if you can hear him,' said the usher. 'Oh, yes,' said the witness, 'perfectly.'

There are many types of witness but each of them has his own individuality, and the first-class advocate endeavours to get on satisfactory terms with him or her as soon as possible. It is, of course, not always possible, and occasionally the judge may intervene during a cross-examination to try to satisfy *himself* as to the nature of the witness. On one such occasion the witness answered most unsatisfactorily a few questions put to him by the judge. The judge paused for a moment and then said:

'Look, Mr X, if you were the judge and I were the witness, and I'd answered your questions as you've answered mine, what would you think?'

'I'd be a bit dubious,' said the witness.

Another witness, who gave a pretty poor account of himself under cross-examination, was also questioned at the end of it by the judge.

'Mr Y,' said the judge, 'you were once a Customs officer, and, I suppose, in that capacity you sometimes questioned people about their luggage?'

'Yes, my Lord.'

'And sometimes, I imagine, they made false statements in answer to your enquiries?'

'Yes, my Lord.'

'And then you would ask them further questions?'

'Yes, my Lord.'

'And sometimes in reply to those further questions they lost their heads and said almost anything, true or false?'

'Yes, my Lord,' said the witness. 'Like I'm doing now.'

At least, those two witnesses were intelligent enough

to know that they had made fools of themselves and
honest enough to admit it.

But it is by no means always counsel who destroys
the witness. He sometimes does it himself. Here is an
example of an expert witness committing harakiri. A
workman had fallen off some scaffolding many years
ago and injured his back. He was off work for some
time and received workmen's compensation. Then he
apparently recovered and went back to work. Some
years later, without any further accident, his back
started to hurt and he was off work again. He claimed
that he was suffering from a slipped disc and that this
was due to his original injury when he fell off the
scaffolding. The employers rejected his claim and
litigation ensued.

The workman called a distinguished surgeon, who
said that he was suffering from a slipped disc and that,
having regard to the history of the case, the strong
probability was that he contracted it at the time of the
accident. That closed the workman's case and the
respondents called as their first witness another distinguished surgeon. He appeared very anxious indeed to
go into the witness box and the reason soon transpired.
There certainly was at that time, and may still be, two
schools of thought in the medical profession about
slipped discs. The surgeon called for the workman was
of one school, the surgeon called for the employers was
obviously of the other. He hardly had time to take the
oath before he launched into an enthusiastic discourse
about slipped discs. He pointed out that many people
alleged to be suffering from slipped discs were suffering
from nothing of the kind. The present, he said, was a

case in point. The workman was not suffering from a slipped disc, the treatment that was being given to him was entirely wrong and he would never get better if it was persisted in. Warming to his work, he explained in somewhat technical terms why his view of the case was right and the other surgeon's wrong. Whether or not the judge understood this explanation is not known but, when the distinguished surgeon paused for a moment, the judge intervened by asking:

'Well, Mr Y, whatever it is the workman is suffering from, how d'you think he got it?'

'Oh,' said the surgeon, 'I expect when he fell on his back.' Collapse of the employer's case. It is difficult to think that the surgeon had expressed that view to the employer's solicitors before, or they would not have proceeded with the case, and one can only imagine that the surgeon became so interested in his lecture on slipped discs, and so pleased to have an apparently interested listener in the judge, that he entirely forgot the object with which he had been called.

But that must be a rare example. Normally expert witnesses are dangerous to cross-examine, unless the cross-examiner really understands the subject matter about which he is cross-examining. For this purpose barristers have from time to time to be electricians, bird-fanciers, chemists, doctors, engineers, architects and even bookmakers. It is true that, if a case is properly prepared, the barrister will have his own client's expert sitting behind him and able to advise him on the spot. But, unless he really understands the questions he is asking, he is unlikely to make much headway. Thus:

'Ask him if it could have been a mutangean cyst,' whispers the expert—or so counsel thinks.

'Could it have been a mutangean cyst?' asks counsel boldly.

'I suppose you mean mutolean cyst,' said the witness. 'No, as far as I know, they are only found in natives of hot climates.'

Counsel cross-examining now has no idea where he is. Was it mutangean or mutolean? What is it anyway? Does it only occur in hot climates? And so forth. He can, of course, ask for a short adjournment to consult with his client, but, if nothing comes of it, this will do more harm than good. The first-class advocate will, as far as is reasonably possible, have covered all the ground over which the case may range and will have fully understood the matters with which he is dealing. It takes a lot of time and is not always simple, but it is easy to recognise the barrister who has really mastered the subject in hand.

The difficulty which judges have with some witnesses is that some of them will vary from the truth to assist their case when it is not necessary to do so. A judge wants to decide a case correctly and, although satisfied that a witness has lied upon one matter, does not want to decide for the other side simply because of that one lie. But it makes the judge's task harder, because he knows that the witness is not entirely reliable. And there are witnesses who are always trying to give cross-examining counsel the answer which the witness thinks he does not want. They are ripe fruit for the experienced cross-examiner who merely has to shake the tree to get what he wants.

The art of cross-examination can only be learned by experience, but the newcomer to the job will find that a gentle cross-examination is always the most effective. Yelling at the witness or abusing him does not endear an advocate to the Court and is unlikely, in most cases, to achieve any satisfactory result with the witness himself. On the other hand, a cross-examination which sends the witness out of the box with the feeling that the counsel against him wasn't such a bad chap after all is by far the most likely to have been successful.

It would be a pity to leave the subject of witnesses without referring to a man who was a party to a case and had been asked some questions which he had answered before being sworn. It was suggested that he should put his answers on oath. He was duly sworn and immediately said:

'Now I'm on oath, I'll tell the truth,' and corrected most of what he'd said before. It cannot be said that every witness has the same respect for the oath, but it is pleasant to record that this particular liar had.

17 *Compromises*

IT IS not always appreciated that most actions never come to trial and are compromised at some stage before the hearing. When it is suggested that all proceedings in an action should be heard in public this factor should be taken into account. It is also not always appreciated that the skilful manœuvring by solicitors and counsel before an action is brought and in its early stages may have a great effect on the result, or may achieve a satisfactory compromise.

Here is a fictitious example of the sort of thing which can happen. One day a Miss Gladys Brain went to see her solicitor. She lived with her sister in the country town of Lyon Keeping and they both took a considerable part in local affairs: the Church, the golf club, the tennis club, the Townswomen's Guild, whist drives, concerts, parties—Mary and Gladys Brain, daughters of the late Lord Brain, were sure to be there. They were both unmarried, and Lyon Keeping and its affairs were their life. Mr Buckram, the Brains' solicitor, was free when Miss Brain called and she was soon shown into his office.

BUCKRAM: Good morning, my dear Miss Brain, so very pleased to see you. Do sit down. If you'll excuse me a minute while I just tie up these papers. My father once lost a client's will by having two sets of papers open at the same time. Yes, he mixed it up with some scheme for a new brewery. It caused a *great* deal of difficulty—oh, dear me, yes. There! Now, what's the trouble?

GLADYS BRAIN: Mr Buckram, I've come about a very serious matter.

BUCKRAM: I'm sorry to hear that.

GLADYS: It's—very serious indeed. A motion is coming before the Committee to expel my sister Mary from the tennis club.

BUCKRAM: Impossible! Whatever for?

GLADYS: Stealing.

BUCKRAM: But that's ridiculous!

GLADYS: Of course it is. But it's terribly worrying all the same. *Please* tell us what we ought to do.

BUCKRAM: Perhaps if you would explain in just a little more detail——

GLADYS: Yes, I'm going to. Well, it seems that some things have been missing from our changing-room at the club during the last few months. So the Committee decided to set a trap.

BUCKRAM: But surely you don't mean to tell me——

GLADYS: Certainly not. But they *think* that Mary fell into it. Of course the whole thing is perfectly ridiculous, as you say, but that's what they think, and they're going to expel her. They're going to hold a special meeting for the purpose. Now, what can we do? It will be ruin for both of us.

BUCKRAM: It must be very worrying for you indeed.

GLADYS: It's more than worrying. It's disastrous. There must be *something we can do*.

BUCKRAM: Well, they can't expel her without giving her a chance to explain.

GLADYS: And suppose they don't accept her explanation? What can we do then?

BUCKRAM: Oh, but I'm sure they will accept her word. After all, it's a monstrous suggestion to make against Miss Brain. When I think of all your father . . .

GLADYS: It *is* monstrous, but that new secretary of ours—Dudley Newington—is prejudiced against her. I know he is, for I went to see him. And he's got the Committee in his pocket.

BUCKRAM: Now, let me see. . . . I think there's only one thing for us to do. We must consult counsel at once. I'll fix an appointment for tomorrow—yes, tomorrow, and you and your sister had better come with me.

So a conference is arranged with a middle-aged and able junior, Mr Larkins, and the next day the two sisters, and Mr Buckram, go up to London to see him. He addresses his questions to Mary Brain.

LARKINS: Please tell me exactly what happened.

GLADYS: My sister went to the changing-room and when she——

LARKINS: Forgive me, Miss Brain, I should prefer to have it from your sister herself.

GLADYS: Oh, very well. Tell them, Mary.

MARY: Well, I went to the changing-room and, when I got there, I couldn't quite remember what I'd gone there for. So I stood for a moment thinking—you know how it is—and then I wandered slowly round the room—still thinking—I've a shocking memory—it wasn't a handkerchief I wanted—I can't even say now what it was. Well, as I went round the room, I just knocked my hand idly against the lockers—you know how one does—and then one of them came open. I was just going to shut it when I happened to see there was some money inside. What a silly thing, I thought, to keep money in a locker and then leave it open—particularly as there have been a few things lost recently—so I just looked in to see how much money there was—so that I could say how much there was if any had been found missing—and I was just counting the money when suddenly Elsie Brown came in. And she gave me such a shock—I dropped all the money.

LARKINS: Well?

MARY: Well, that's all really.

LARKINS: Did you help to pick it up?

MARY: No, I didn't as a matter of fact.

LARKINS: What did you do?

MARY: I just went out.

LARKINS: Didn't you say anything?

MARY: I did say something about it being silly to leave all that money about.

LARKINS: But why didn't you help to pick it up?

MARY: I don't know really. It gave me such a shock —Elsie coming in like that.

LARKINS: Why? You were doing nothing wrong.

MARY: I'm nervous by nature. And then I suppose I suddenly thought she might think I was taking it . . . I got confused.

GLADYS: She lost her head.

LARKINS: I must ask you this, Miss Brain. Please understand that I'm not intending to be offensive, but

I must ask the question. Were you intending to steal any of that money?

MARY: Oh, no! I didn't need it. We're very comfortably off.

LARKINS: You're quite sure?

GLADYS: Of course she's quite sure. The whole thing is preposterous.

LARKINS: What is the next you heard of the matter?

GLADYS: We heard nothing until Mary had this notice telling her of the motion to expel her and inviting her to attend the meeting.

LARKINS: I see that that notice was a week ago.

GLADYS: Yes. In the meantime I tried to see Mr Newington, the secretary, but he avoided me. However, I did eventually buttonhole him.

LARKINS: What happened?

GLADYS: It was very unpleasant.

LARKINS: Why? What did he say?

GLADYS: Well, I started off by asking him what he meant by accusing my sister, and he said: 'She's been doing it for years.' I said: 'How dare you!' and he replied: 'I'm very sorry, Miss Brain, but your sister's been stealing one thing after another for a long time. We never knew who it was till now.' So I went straight round to Mr Buckram.

LARKINS: I see. Now, tell me, have you ever stolen anything in Lyon Keeping?

MARY: But——

GLADYS: Of course she hasn't. She told you—we're quite comfortably off. The suggestion is absurd.

LARKINS: Tell me this. Would you be prepared to risk a criminal prosecution?

GLADYS: A prosecution?

LARKINS: Yes. You see, it's pretty obvious that they don't intend to prosecute or they'd have done so before; they simply propose to expel your sister from the club and forget the matter.

GLADYS: That's easy enough for them, but . . .

LARKINS: I quite agree. Now, I have an almost child-like belief in our system of justice—in this sense—that I don't believe innocent people are ordinarily convicted of serious crime. My advice to you, if you're innocent, is to challenge the Committee to prosecute you. They may do so, they may not. Probably they won't, but they might. And it's you who'll be taking the risk, not me.

GLADYS: But a prosecution! It would be horrible. All the publicity!

LARKINS: If your sister is expelled from the club, it'll be just as bad, won't it? Life would be intolerable for you both.

BUCKRAM: Very true, Mr Larkins, very true. In a town like ours . . .

GLADYS: Forgive me, Mr Buckram; I want to know what this is leading to, Mr Larkins.

LARKINS: I'll tell you. Your object is to prevent your sister from being expelled. Now, a club committee is perfectly entitled to expel a member provided it acts fairly and within the rules. Accordingly, provided it gave her a fair hearing, the Committee could say it was satisfied that Miss Brain was guilty—even if the magistrates or a jury would say not guilty. We've got to try to stop the Committee dealing with the case. If you take my advice, Mr Buckram's firm will at once write

a letter to Mr Newington in terms which I shall draft.
Now, will you take the risk if I challenge them to
prosecute?

GLADYS: You advise that we should?

LARKINS: You'd be unwise not to do so—unless, of
course, Miss Brain is guilty. Only she knows that for
certain.

Eventually the sisters decide to take the risk with the
result that two days later Mr Newington receives this
letter:

We have been consulted by our client, the Honourable
Mary Brain, in regard to a very serious slander uttered by
you to her sister.

The letter then sets out the conversation between
Gladys and Mr Newington:

Unless we receive an unreserved and unqualified withdrawal of these monstrous charges for which you have no
grounds whatsoever, our instructions are to issue a writ for
slander. The remainder of this letter is written to you as
secretary of the Lyon Keeping Tennis Club.

The letter then goes on to deal with the proposed
expulsion and, while asserting in very clear terms her
innocence, challenges the Committee to prosecute her:

It would be a grave injustice if, without giving our client
an opportunity of being vindicated in open Court, you try
her behind closed doors where the rules of evidence which
protect innocent people will not be observed. If our client
is guilty, of course she should be expelled from the club,

but it will be monstrous to deny her the opportunity of clearing herself. If the Committee considers she is guilty, let them institute a prosecution—let them not be judge and jury and prosecution too.

Mr Newington is alarmed by this letter and takes it to a solicitor friend, George Brighton.

NEWINGTON: Well, what do I do, George? I'm hanged if I'll apologise. The woman's a crook.

BRIGHTON: Slander actions are expensive.

NEWINGTON: It's bluff, if you ask me. It's all part of a scheme to stop this expulsion.

BRIGHTON: You're probably right there.

NEWINGTON: Now what about this prosecution business?

BRIGHTON: It's a risk. You see, if you prosecute and fail, you can't very well expel her then. If you succeeded of course you'd be all right.

NEWINGTON: But you don't think we should succeed, unless you've changed your mind since we consulted you in the first place.

BRIGHTON: No, I don't think you would. You see, suspicion isn't enough—and you can't bring the other losses into it.

NEWINGTON: But she dropped the money and ran. Surely that's good enough?

BRIGHTON: She didn't run. She stayed in the club—*and* she told one of the members what had happened. She is a nervous person, she might have lost her head—thought she'd be suspected. It takes a great deal to convict a person of good character of stealing.

NEWINGTON: Well, if we don't prosecute?

BRIGHTON: You can expel her just the same—after a proper hearing before the Committee, of course. She can't stop you doing that. But she can sue you for slander. You were an ass to open your mouth so wide.

NEWINGTON: Well, it's done now. What do you advise?

BRIGHTON: If you want to be sure of getting her out of the club, don't prosecute—give her a fair hearing and expel her. And let the slander rip for a moment. In fact, I think I should wait until after the Committee Meeting before doing anything. It's only a few days. One doesn't have to answer a letter like that by return.

Accordingly no answer is received by Mr Buckram, and he telephones Mr Larkins to know what to do.

BUCKRAM: The meeting's on Monday. It looks as though they're going through with it.

LARKINS: Yes, it does. You'd better come and see me at once and bring your client with you.

So on the afternoon of the same day, which was a Friday, Mr Buckram and the two sisters take the train to London.

GLADYS: It's very inconvenient going up to town at such short notice.

BUCKRAM: I'm very sorry, Miss Brain, but, if I may say so, it would be more inconvenient if your sister were expelled on Monday.

MARY: Oh dear! I can't bear the thought of it. How could I walk through the streets? Everyone would point at me—and at you, Gladys.

GLADYS: There's no need to remind me of that. Does Mr Larkins think he can stop it?

BUCKRAM: He's a very able man and I'm sure he wouldn't send for us like this if there weren't something we could do.

Eventually the three of them see Mr Larkins once again in his chambers in the Temple.

LARKINS: There's no time to be lost, Mr Buckram. You must issue a writ for slander at once against Mr Newington.

BUCKRAM: Will you settle it, please, Mr Larkins? I don't want there to be any slip-up.

LARKINS: I've already done so as a matter of fact, and I've also drafted an affidavit to be sworn by Miss Mary Brain. You must get it sworn this afternoon.

GLADYS: But how is all this going to stop the meeting on Monday?

LARKINS: I'll tell you. Tomorrow morning we shall apply to the judge in chambers for an order to stop the meeting being held pending the trial of the action.

BUCKRAM: But how can we do that? The Committee isn't even a party to the action.

LARKINS: Quite right. It isn't. We shall ask the Court to prevent the Committee holding its meeting until after the case is heard on the ground that, if it is held, it may prejudice the fair trial of the action between Miss Brain and Mr Newington.

GLADYS: How could it do that?

LARKINS: Well, for example, the decision of the Committee may be known all over the country.

MARY: All over the country?

LARKINS: In view of your position, I'm afraid so. But that helps us as far as this application is concerned, because a jury in any part of the country might be prejudiced by the knowledge that the plaintiff had been convicted by her fellow members. Then, again, the evidence of witnesses may be affected by the questions they are asked by the Committee or by knowledge of the Committee's finding. I don't pretend it's a strong case, but if you undertake not to use the club until the action has been heard, it won't do any real harm to the club to have the meeting postponed, whereas if they hold the meeting and expel you, it may affect your action.

BUCKRAM: Do you think we'll get the order?

LARKINS: With luck we should get it tomorrow—as long as you get the writ issued and the affidavit sworn today. So meet me tomorrow here at half past ten.

GLADYS: Tomorrow! But it's Saturday!

LARKINS: Yes. But there's always a judge available—we'll have to go to his home.

And so the next day Mr Larkins and Mr Buckram call on Mr Justice Broad, the judge in chambers.

LARKINS: Here is the writ and affidavit, my Lord. It's a slightly unusual application, but it's very urgent. It's to restrain a contempt of court.

BROAD: Let me look. I see. A claim for slander—and you want an injunction against the Club Committee who aren't being sued. Can I do this?

LARKINS: Yes, my Lord. I thought your Lordship might like to see an authority on the subject. So I've brought one.

BROAD: Why must you have an order now?

LARKINS: There's no time for a summons. The

meeting's on Monday. Your Lordship will see that in paragraph 4 of the affidavit.

BROAD: But suppose the members don't want your client hanging about the club?

LARKINS: My client is quite prepared to undertake not to go to the club until after the action is disposed of.

BROAD: Let me see the authority you've brought. Yes—I follow. Well, if your client gives that undertaking, I don't think it can do any harm if I give you an order until Tuesday. You must serve the summons on Monday.

LARKINS: That will be done, my Lord.

So Mr Buckram takes the next train back from London, and on Monday morning he ensures that Mr Newington is served with the writ for slander and that he and all the members of the Committee are served with the judge's order restraining the Committee from holding its meeting on Monday. In consequence, Mr Newington telephones the other members of the Committee and then goes round to see his solicitor and shows him the documents.

NEWINGTON: What do we do now?

BRIGHTON: We'll have to instruct counsel at once. There won't be time to deal with the matter by Tuesday. We'll get an adjournment until Friday, and we'll have to give an undertaking until then.

Next day, Mr Newington and Mr Brighton call on their counsel, Mr Grimes, and explain the case to him.

BRIGHTON: I've agreed to an adjournment until next Friday to give you time to consider the matter. What's your first reaction?

GRIMES: Tell me, my dear fellow, does it matter to

your people if the meeting's postponed until after the action's heard?

NEWINGTON: We'd prefer to get on with it.

GRIMES: Of course you would, but if she keeps away from the club, how will it hurt you?

NEWINGTON: We'd like to get it over and done with. It's a nasty thing to have hanging over us.

GRIMES: Well, we shall see, my dear fellow, we shall see.

Eventually they do see. Mr Justice Broad, after going into the matter at length, finally decides that on the whole it will be fairer to have the meeting postponed until after the trial of the action. As the action gets nearer trial the defendant, Mr Newington, is getting worried about finance.

NEWINGTON: I do think the Committee ought to contribute *something*. It's your battle I'm fighting.

1ST MEMBER: My dear boy—I sympathise, but with the school fees and Lucy's operation, I'm afraid . . .

2ND MEMBER: After all we didn't tell you to make wholesale allegations of theft against the woman.

NEWINGTON: You've all said the same thing.

1ST MEMBER: That's another matter. It can't be proved against us; you said it to her sister. That was asking for trouble.

NEWINGTON: D'you realise this whole affair may cost me a thousand pounds or more in costs alone?

1ST MEMBER: We're most awfully sorry, old boy. Very bad luck.

NEWINGTON: Well, I'm fed to the teeth with the whole thing.

Which is exactly what Mr Larkins intended. A few

days after the abortive Committee Meeting, Mr Brighton sends for Mr Newington.

BRIGHTON: Good news. They've got the wind-up.

NEWINGTON: Oh? What makes you think that?

BRIGHTON: We've had a letter from them. Listen to this. 'Without prejudice. As you are aware, our client's only concern is to protect her good name. She has never desired damages. Accordingly, before delivering our brief to counsel, we desire to give your client an opportunity of making a full and unreserved apology and withdrawal in terms to be approved by us and to be published in the local Press. Should you be prepared to make such withdrawal, our client will not even require you to pay her costs, appreciating that her financial position is better than your own.' What do you think of that?

NEWINGTON: If you ask me, it's a good offer, let's take it.

BRIGHTON: Take it? But if you do that you'll have to admit that she hasn't stolen a thing, and the Committee can't possibly expel her after an admission like that by its secretary.

NEWINGTON: I dare say not. But if they want to expel her they should share the cost. All they were prepared to risk were the five half-crowns they put in Elsie Brown's locker.

BRIGHTON: I see your point. But if you ask me, it's just a last throw. She's frightened to go on with it and if you hold firm she'll cave in. She's obviously terrified of going into the witness box.

NEWINGTON: I hope you're right.

BRIGHTON: She'll never go into Court. You'll see.

The next thing we'll get will be a notice of discontinuance. Shouldn't be surprised if we get it within the week. Not asking for damages or costs!

NEWINGTON: It does look a bit phoney, I agree. All right, turn it down and see what happens.

BRIGHTON: I'll warn them that we are delivering the brief to counsel.

That friendly hint is to tell Miss Brain's solicitors that, if they discontinue at once, it will cost them less. But they do not take the hint, briefs are delivered to counsel and eventually the day of the trial arrives.

NEWINGTON: You said she wouldn't go into court!

BRIGHTON: It may just be bluff. She hasn't gone into the witness box yet. They may be waiting for *us* to crack.

NEWINGTON: That's exactly what I feel like doing— after that last cheque I gave you.

BRIGHTON: D'you want to ask if their offer's still open?

NEWINGTON: What d'you advise?

BRIGHTON: Well, if you don't want to take the risk of losing, I'll tell Grimes to make the offer at the last possible moment, but to see if they crack first.

NEWINGTON: All right. We've gone so far now, I expect you're right. I wish we'd taken her offer in the first place.

BRIGHTON: Sorry, old boy; these things will happen.

And so on a Monday in June . . .

ASSOCIATE: Brain against Newington.

LARKINS: May it please your Lordship, members of the jury, the plaintiff in this case is the Honourable Mary Brain and the defendant is Mr Dudley Newington. The plaintiff's claim against the defendant is for damages for slander spoken by the defendant in August last.

GRIMES: Larkins!

LARKINS: Yes.

GRIMES (*In an undertone—to Larkins*): I'll take your offer, if it's still open.

LARKINS: Will your Lordship forgive me a moment? (*In an undertone*): Full withdrawal and apology in open Court, and in the local Press.

GRIMES: Yes—but no damages or costs.

LARKINS: But nothing to be said about that in Court.

GRIMES: Agreed.

LARKINS: I must apologise to your Lordship, but I am now happy to tell your Lordship that your Lordship and the jury will no longer be troubled with the case. The defendant desires to make a full and unreserved withdrawal of all the allegations and to apologise for having made them and to state in open Court that there was no foundation for any of them.

So, at the last moment, Mr Larkins' strategy is triumphant. The one thing that his client wanted was to have her character cleared. He had obtained instructions to settle on those terms at any time. He thought they would in the end prove too tempting for Mr Newington to resist, and he was right. A day or two afterwards in Lyon Keeping the Committee meet.

NEWINGTON: Well, it's agreed then that this motion to expel is dropped.

1ST MEMBER: It'll have to be. Better have all the locks changed.

NEWINGTON: I shouldn't bother. She won't do it again, now.

And in the home of Gladys and Mary Brain:

MARY: What a *relief*! I can hardly believe that it's all over.

GLADYS: H'm. It'll be some time before it's all forgotten. Still I'm thankful we've got you out of it. And now we have, you'd better tell me. Did you?

MARY: Oh, Gladys—you know you said yourself we were comfortably off, and I'd no need to.

N

18 *In Camera*

THERE has been some discussion in the Press about the fact that certain proceedings are heard in private and complaints have been made that this offends against the rule that cases should be heard in public, unless there is some special reason to the contrary. Most people are aware that, when actions are brought in the High Court, there may be all kinds of applications made by the parties before the action is finally heard in open Court. It is often against the interests of both parties that anything should be heard of the case in public at that early stage. Such publicity might prevent an early compromise or it might injure both parties. And, as long as the action itself is heard in public, it does not appear that the public interest suffers by reason of the privacy allowed for these early stages in action.

But the odd thing is that there is no consistency in these matters by the Courts themselves. For example, an application for an injunction pending the trial of an action is heard in private in the Queen's Bench Division, but in public in the Chancery Division. In most cases a plaintiff can choose whichever Court suits him better. The defendant has no choice in the matter. So, if the plaintiff wants early publicity, he brings his action in the Chancery Division. If he wants to avoid publicity he brings it in the Queen's Bench

Division. But if the defendant wants publicity and the plaintiff brings the action in the Queen's Bench Division the defendant can obtain publicity a little later, if the judge has decided against him, by appealing from the decision to the Court of Appeal.

All cases are normally heard by the Court of Appeal in open Court, and it is not particularly obvious why privacy should be ensured for the application before the judge but not before the Court of Appeal. If it is desirable in the one case surely it is equally desirable in the other?

It would appear that until recently no one has worried very much about the situation. Lawyers have known what the position is and advised their clients accordingly.

Few litigants or lawyers would dispute that the interests of civil litigation are best served by privacy being permitted in the initial stages and publicity being reserved for the trial only. They would probably agree that it would serve the interests of the litigants if this applied equally to applications which went as far as the Court of Appeal. There are, of course, cases where one side or the other or both sides want publicity. For example, a plaintiff who claims that he has been libelled may want it to be widely known that he has taken proceedings. But these are probably the exceptional cases, and most litigants would prefer to get on with the preliminary skirmishes prior to the trial without the public's eye being upon them. Indeed, many of them would no doubt prefer a trial in private altogether but they recognise that in the general interest this cannot be done.

If the right principle is that private litigation is to be under the eyes of the public, it may be a little difficult logically to defend the privacy permitted to the stages of an action before it comes to trial. But, if the lack of publicity smooths the paths of litigation and makes compromises easier, the advantages to the parties would appear to outweigh any advantage in principle the public may gain by compelling them to wash their legal linen in public from the very beginning.

There is, too, a very special type of action which, it is to be hoped, will always be allowed privacy in its initial stages. These are the actions where a person has been blackmailed and is bringing an action to restrain the blackmailer from continuing his persecution. The Criminal Courts normally permit such a person to be known as Mr X, and the Press has never at any time complained at this indulgence. On the contrary. But, although a person may be called Mr X, many people cannot help learning his real identity. He has to give evidence and must be seen at least by all those concerned in the case and probably by a good many other people too. It cannot, therefore, be long before his identity becomes known fairly widely. And that is the blackmailer's weapon. That is very probably why only a small proportion of those who are blackmailed ever dare to seek the aid of the Criminal Courts. They know that, however helpful the Courts and the Press may be, their identity at the very least *may* become known to the persons from whom they want to keep their secret. Now the view may be taken by some people that people who are blackmailed deserve their punishment. If they had not done anything wrong, they could not be blackmailed. That is no doubt true in the vast majority of cases, though from time to time a completely innocent person, who fears that he may be believed guilty of some misdeed or impropriety, yields to the threats of the blackmailer. But few people take the view that a person who is being blackmailed deserves no pity and, on the contrary, it is generally agreed that blackmail is one of the worst crimes and that, as far as possible, every assistance should be given to a person to get out of the blackmailer's clutches, even though the victim has been guilty of some offence or impropriety.

Now in many of these cases the civil law can give a person more protection than the criminal law. This is because of the privacy which is available to applications which are made in the course of an action. If a person who has got into the hands of a blackmailer comes to an agreement with the blackmailer that, in return for payment of a certain sum the blackmailer will neither carry out his threat, whatever it was, nor approach his victim again for money, that agreement can be enforced by the Courts by injunction. And, as long as this can be done without publicity, the blackmailer can be effectively silenced.

What happens in such a case is this. Blackmailers are nearly always ready to promise that they won't ask again, simply because they know (or think) that they can break their promises as often as they like and that there is nothing that the victims can do about it. So there should not be much difficulty in persuading a blackmailer to make an agreement of the kind mentioned, either in writing or by word of mouth.

As soon as the blackmailer breaks the agreement by asking for more, a writ is issued against him and, at the same time, an application is made in private to the judge in chambers to restrain the blackmailer from breaking the agreement in any way. The victim need not appear on the application and the only persons who will know anything about it are his own legal advisers and the judge and certain Court officials. Now a blackmailer knows that once a person goes to the Courts the game is up and accordingly he does not want the action to be brought to a public hearing. It is true that, if it were brought to trial, the plaintiff might be ruined, but the judge would send the papers to the Director of Public Prosecutions with a view to the defendant's prosecution. Once, therefore, an injunction has been obtained, the victim is probably completely safe. But, should the blackmailer break the injunction, and, in spite of it, seek to obtain more money from the plaintiff, he will be liable to be sent to prison for an indefinite period. And all this will be done without any publicity whatever.

Now recently there has been complaint that people can be sent to prison in this manner, and the law will probably be changed both so that applications to send people to prison for contempt of court shall be made in public and to ensure that they can appeal from any such order for their imprisonment. But it is certainly to be hoped that, in a case of blackmail, the present procedure will remain available. There could be quite sufficient safeguards to see that it was not abused. But, if no such provision is made, then the one method by which the victim of blackmail may be able to extricate himself from his appalling circumstances will have been taken away.

The only other cases where hearings are now and should remain in private are cases where the custody of children is concerned, or the like. But there is no controversy about these.

19 *Conclusion*

DELAY and inconvenience, uncertainty and expense. At the beginning of this book it was stated that these were the main defects of any system of law. It has been impossible to deal with all the detailed workings of the law where improvement can be made. In the conduct of an action, for example, it may be possible still further to reduce the steps which each side has to take before the trial without prejudicing the fair trial of the action. Matters of this kind are being considered all the time and periodically new rules are formulated to achieve this object. For example, the Rules of the Supreme Court are being revised at the present moment. But, apart from this type of improvement, it has appeared that the remedy for nearly all the most serious defects in the workings of our law lies in public expenditure. And each time the question is whether the country can afford it.

The building of new courts and the appointment of additional judges and magistrates would inevitably remove the greater part of the delays and inconveniences at present suffered by litigants, lawyers and witnesses. The introduction of a system by which doubtful questions of law were decided by the Court *before* parties have to litigate about them at great expense would do something to remove uncertainty. The acceptance by the State of some liability for the costs of litigation would reduce the cost to the individual. But all these reforms may be considered luxuries which the public cannot yet afford. At least, however, they should be weighed against the various other items of public expenditure.

One suggested reform which would not require the expenditure of public money is the transfer of a greater part of the burden of costs from the winning to the losing party in litigation. Provided a litigant is not extravagant in his conduct of an action he ought, in the ordinary way, to be entitled to recover all his costs against the losing party, including the costs of legal advice and correspondence occurring before the proceedings have started. It appears an obvious injustice that, even though his unsuccessful opponent is able to meet the bill, the law does not require him to do so. This defect in the law is by no means limited to this country and, indeed, in some other countries it is even more glaring. The fact that safeguards would have to be made to prevent one party deliberately increasing the costs of an action, so as to deter his opponent from contesting it, is no reason why the present unsatisfactory situation should be allowed to continue. It could, for example, be laid down that indemnity should be the principle but that unjustifiable extravagances should be disallowed.

But, however much reforms may improve the standard of English justice, the wise man will always avoid being caught up in litigation if he can possibly do so. And on rather different principles the criminal will always avoid being caught as long as he can. But these facts should not deter those connected with the law from trying to make the experience of litigation as pleasant as the nature of the case permits. For one thing, the seats should be more comfortable. At the moment the Old Bailey is about the only court in London where counsel, solicitors, witnesses and jury-men can sit in comfort. But that is a detail. It will be a great day for English justice when the only complaint which can be made about it is that the seats in most of the Courts are too hard.

Index